Art environments are the bearing of its creator's soul.

Art Environments are the creations of people who step beyond the simple birdhouse, flag or pillows on the outdoor furniture to the point of decorating their personal surrounding spaces to attract the public's attention.

They may be created with deeply personal reasons, but the public display is the call for attention through the creation. The reasons for such amazing personal expansive décor can be to share the art, a conduit for a message, sooth a lonely spirit, or a dive in to deal with a tragedy through the healing process and a focused mind.

Tim Kerr and his lovely wife, Beth have long sought out art environments and the hopeful chance of meeting their creators. They are inspired by the artists and their drive to create. Each place is created under different circumstances but with a purpose to bring satisfaction and comfort within its magnificence.

Tim's photographs have documented these places and shown slices of the beauty of the human spirit. His paintings of the creators are a tribute including a quote by the artists. These places can be like flower gardens and only exist for limited time, so documentation is honoring the creative process.

Tim's own work is always signed "your name here" which shares the character of the art environment artist and obviously his common thread of interest in these special places. Sharing the message . . . you can do this.

— Julie Webb
Webb Gallery, Waxahachie TX

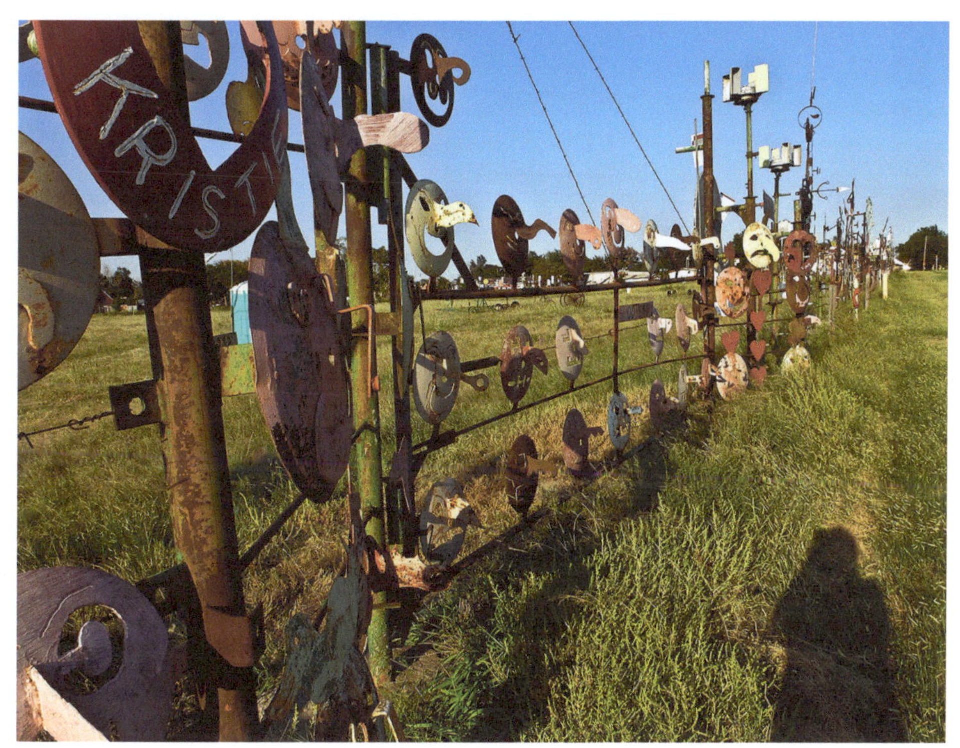

self expression

can be found anywhere and everywhere.
Open up your five senses to be aware of
your own, and others' celebrations. And
always remember that you
can color outside the
lines.

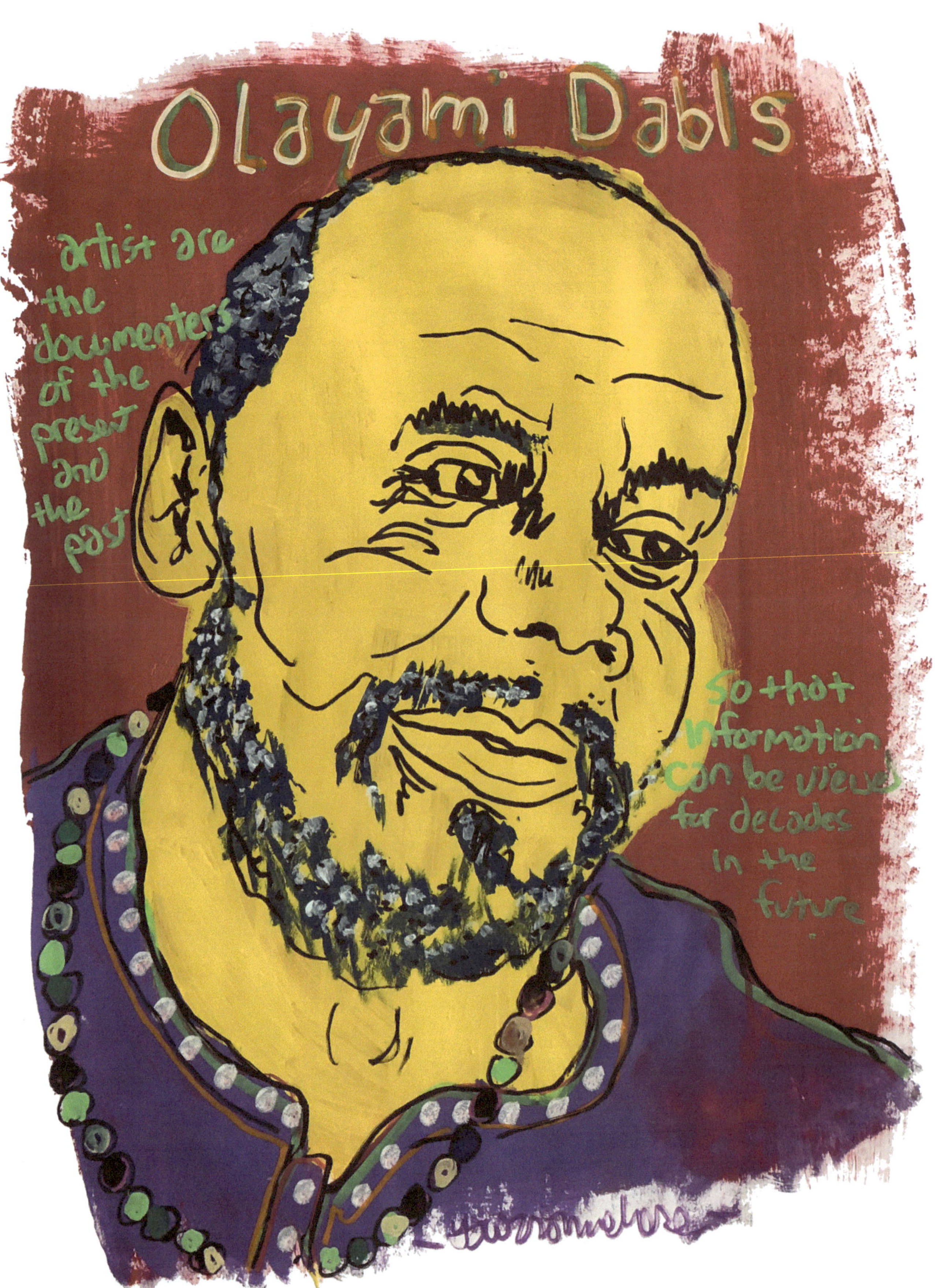

Olayami Dabls

artist are the documenters of the present and the past

so that information can be viewed for decades in the future

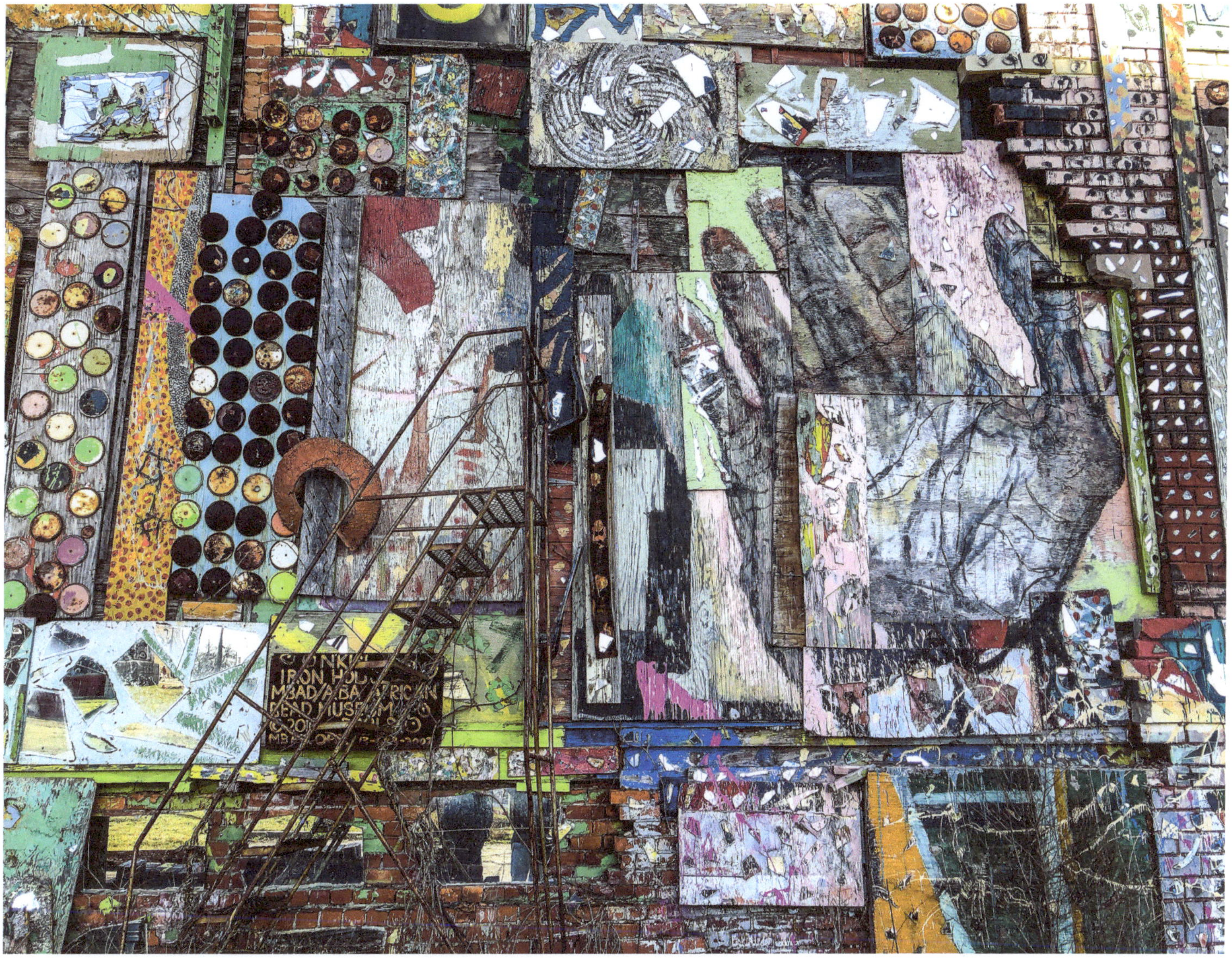

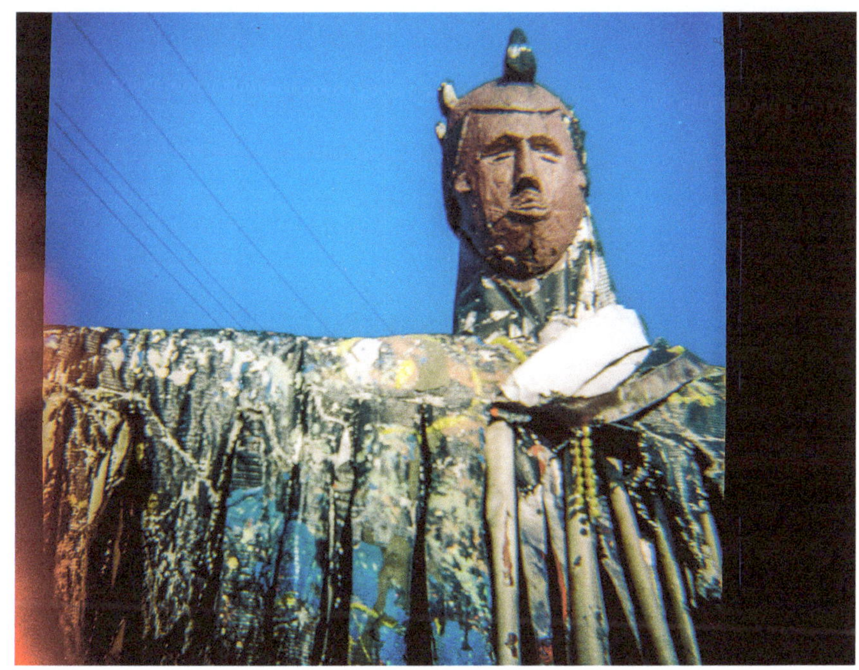
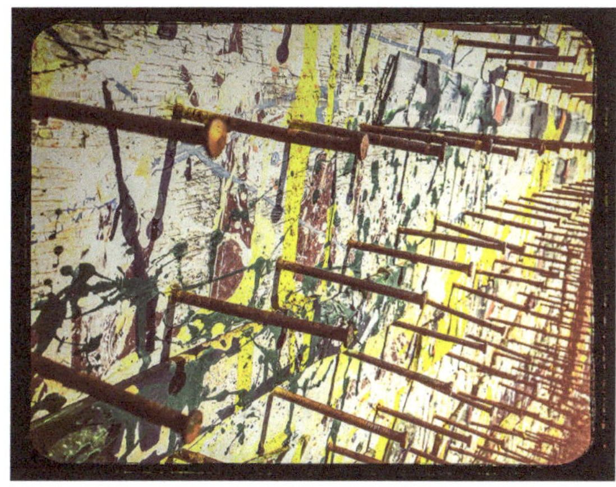

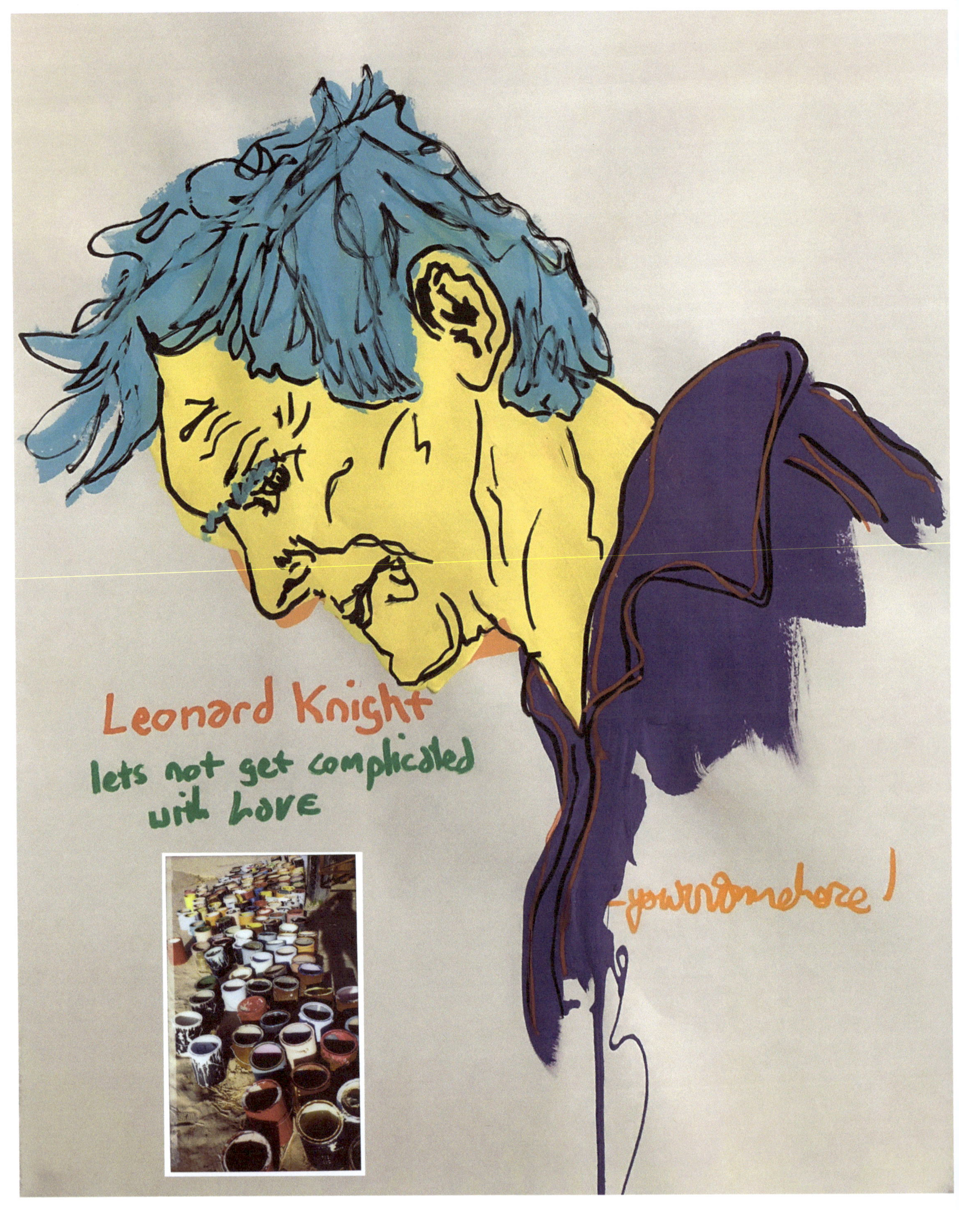

Leonard Knight
lets not get complicated
with Love

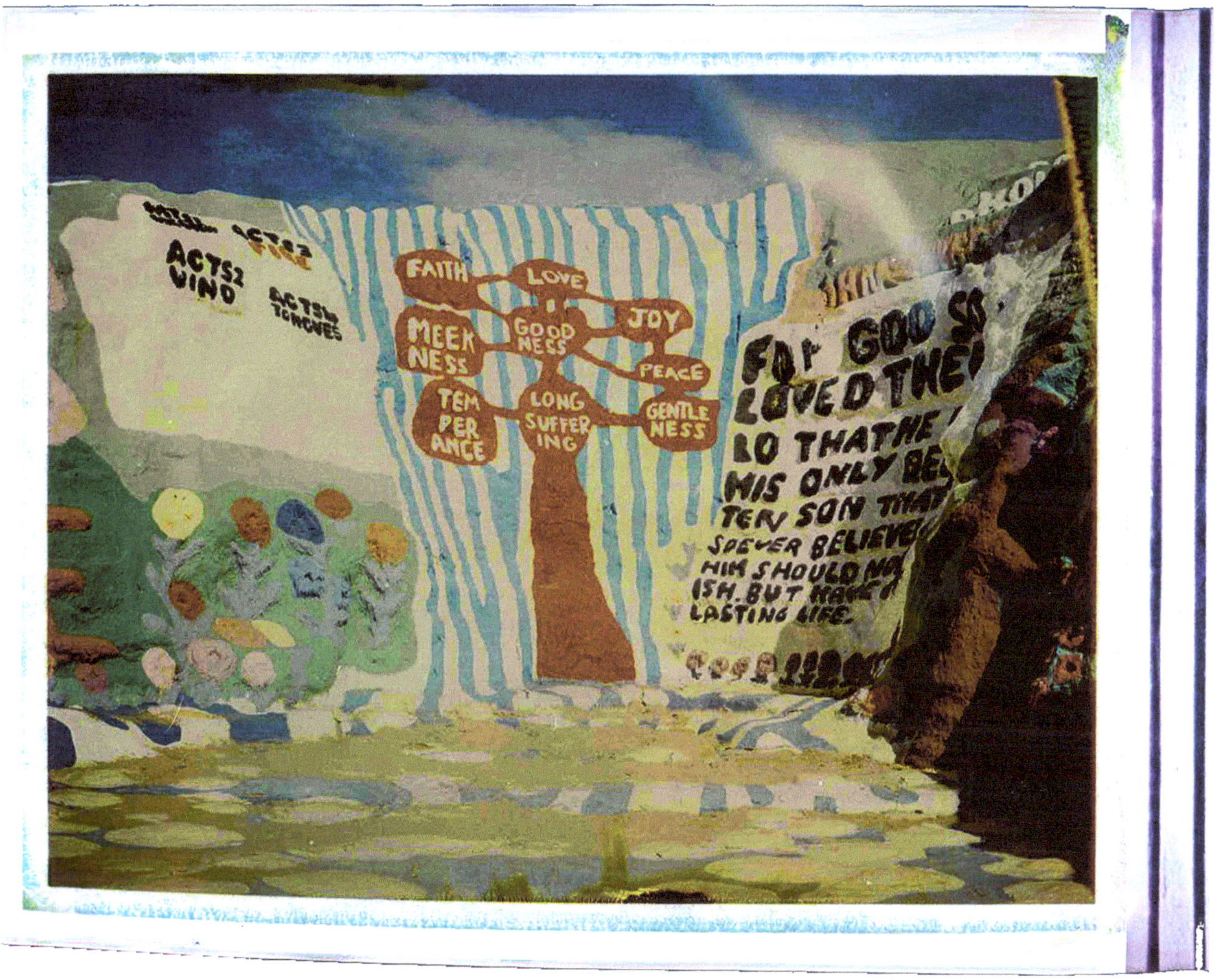

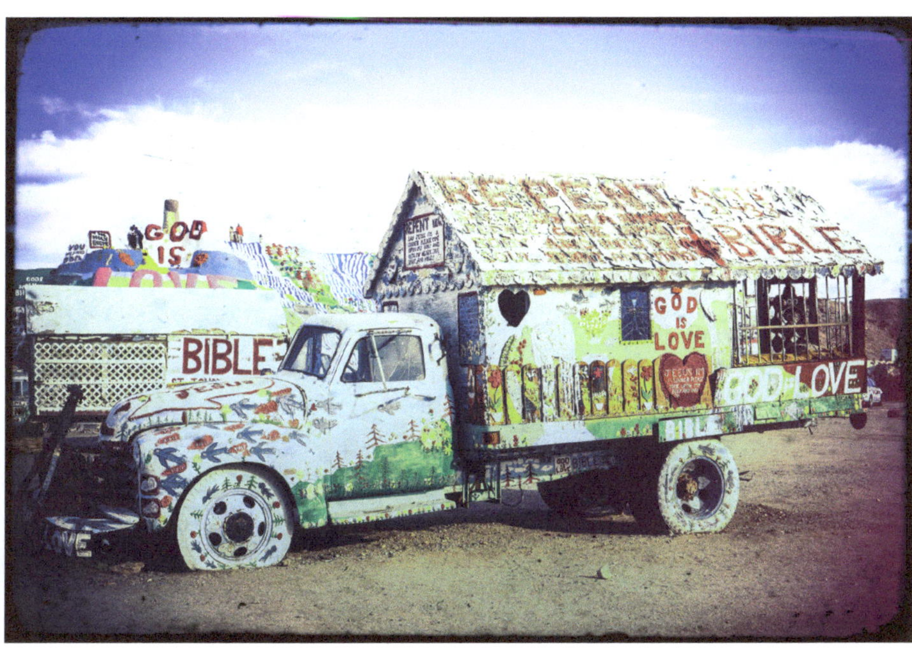

GOD IS LOVE
BIBLE
GOD IS LOVE
GOD LOVE
BIBLE
REPENT

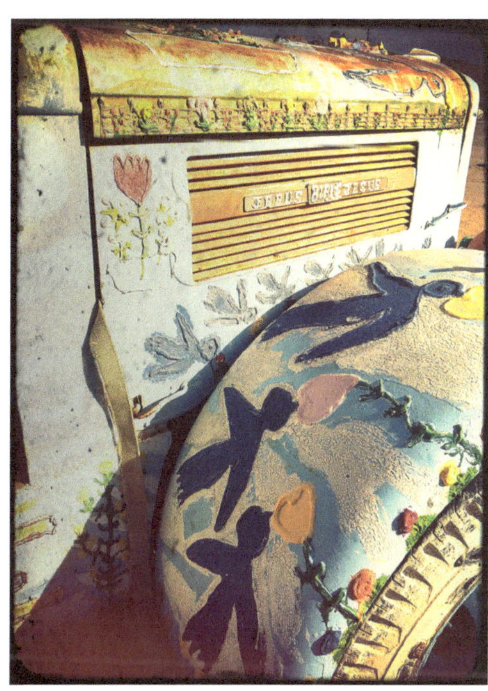

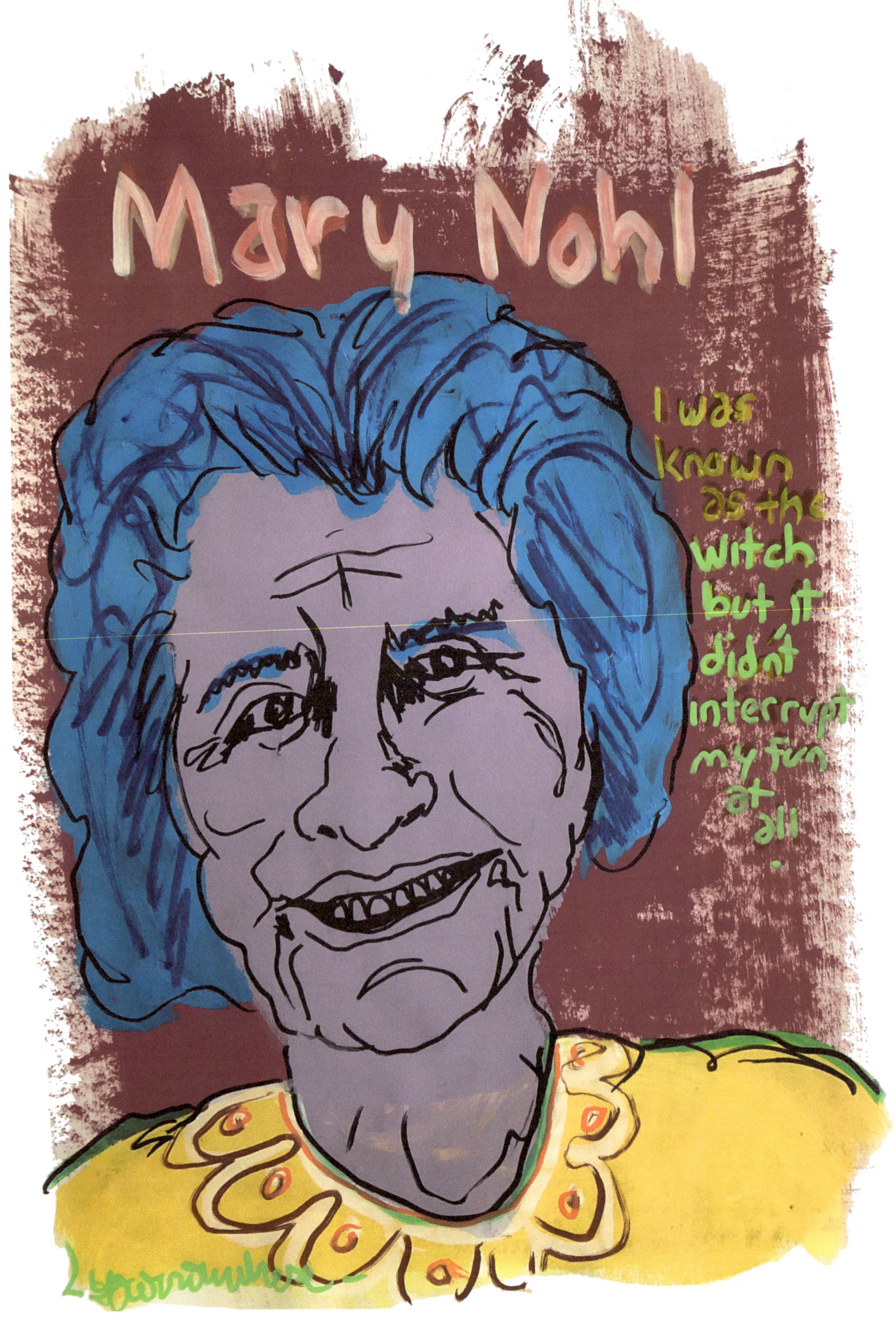

Mary Nohl
I was known as the witch but it didn't interrupt my fun at all

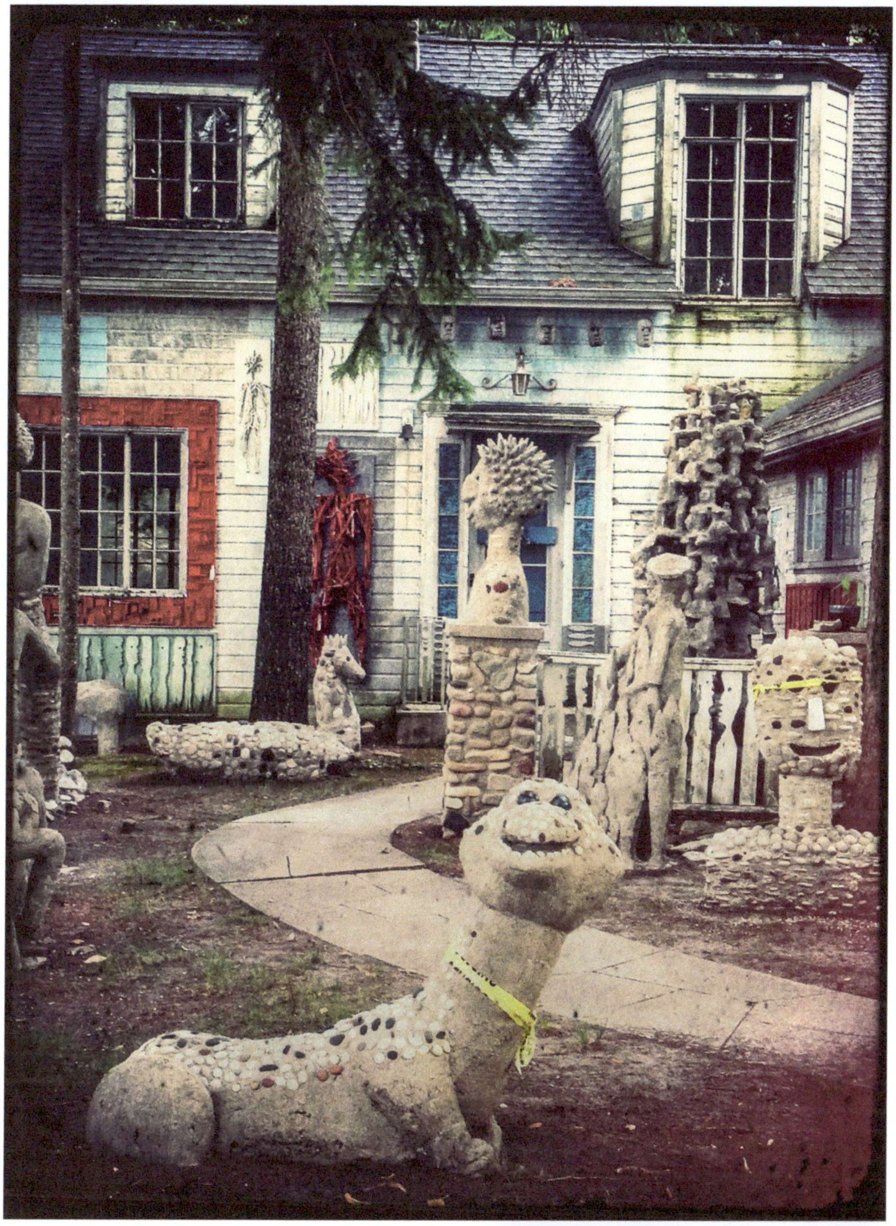

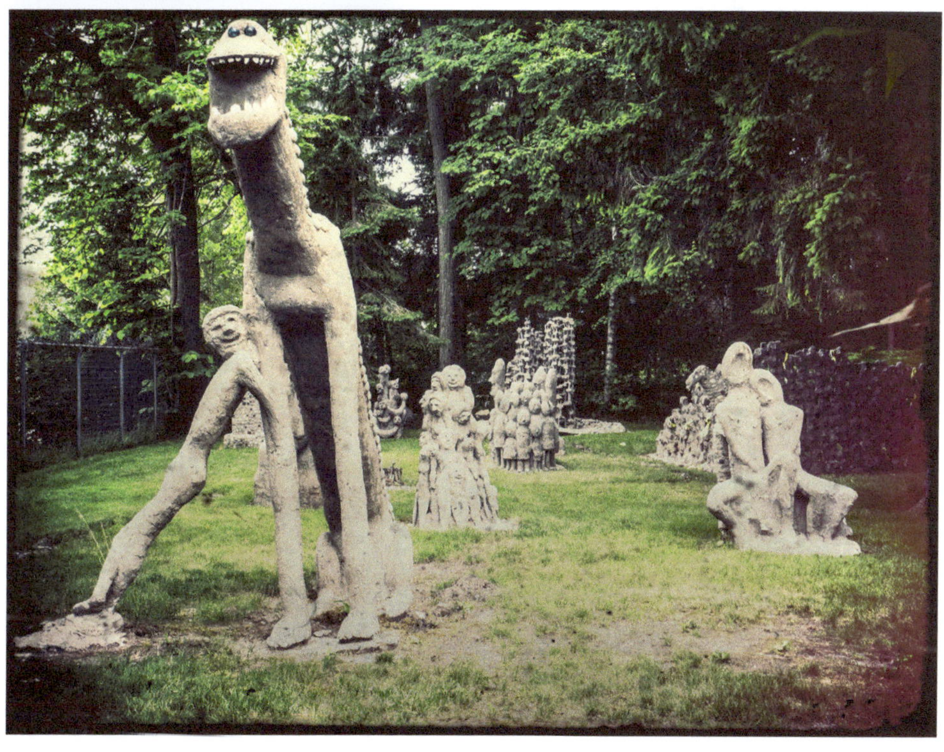

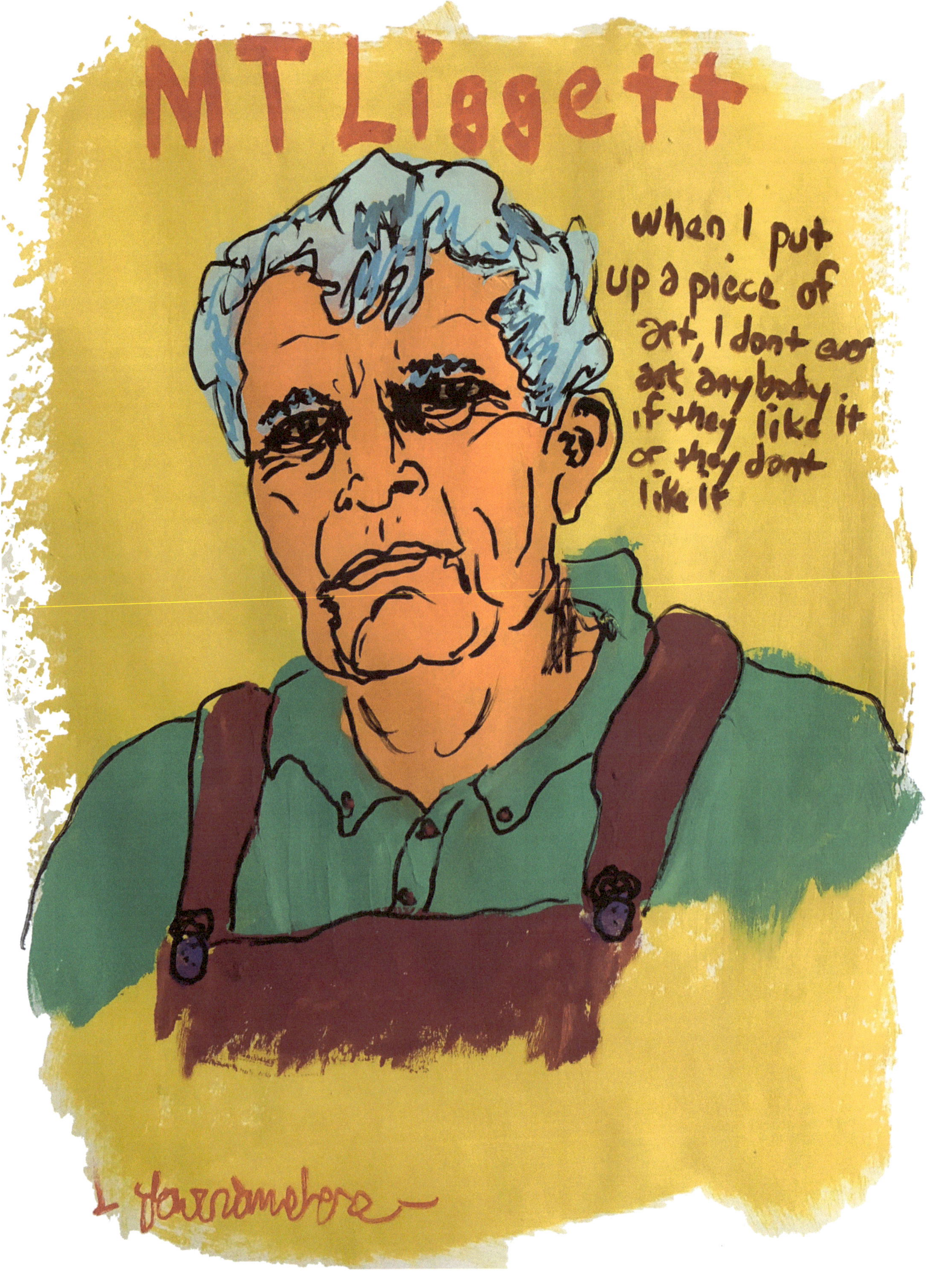
MT Liggett
when I put up a piece of art, I don't ever ask anybody if they like it or they dont like it

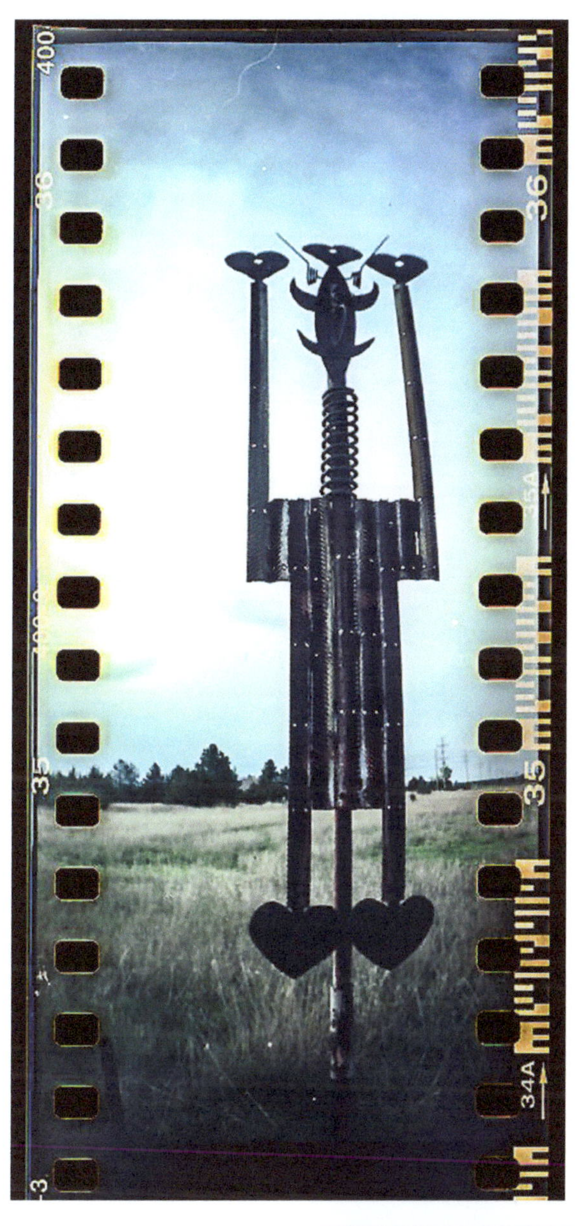
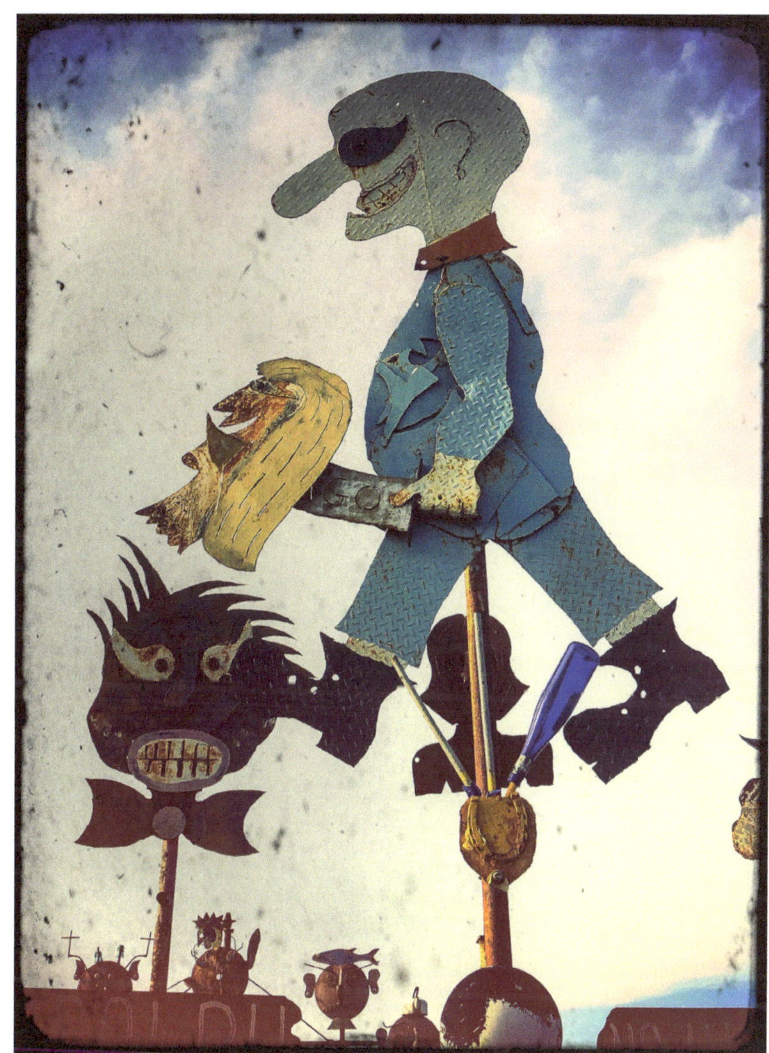
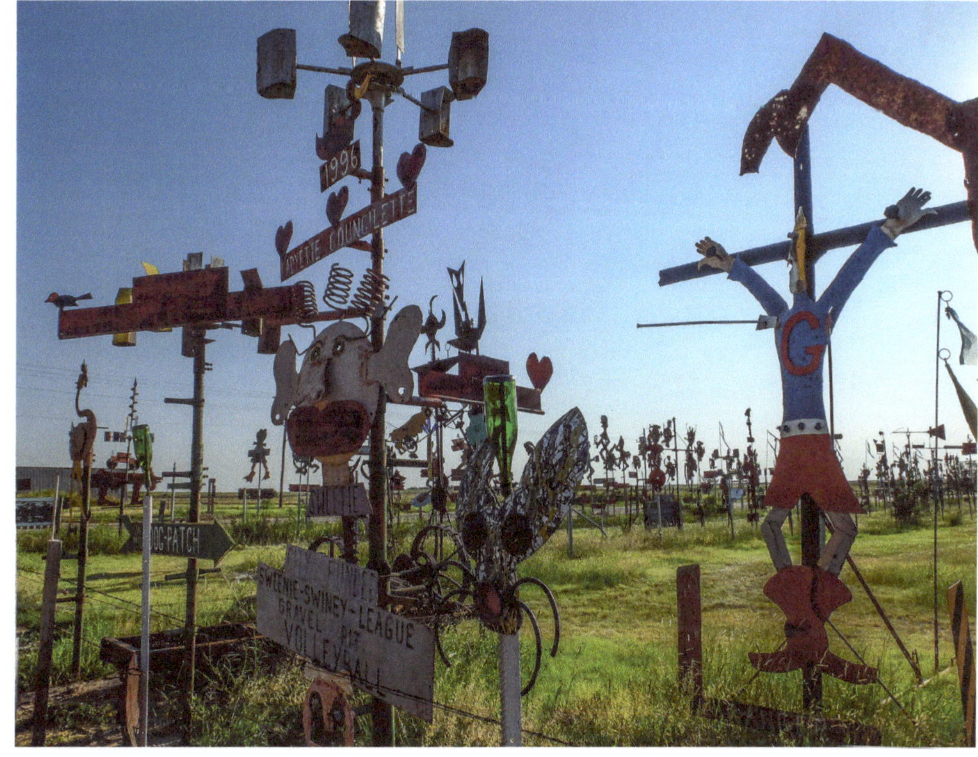

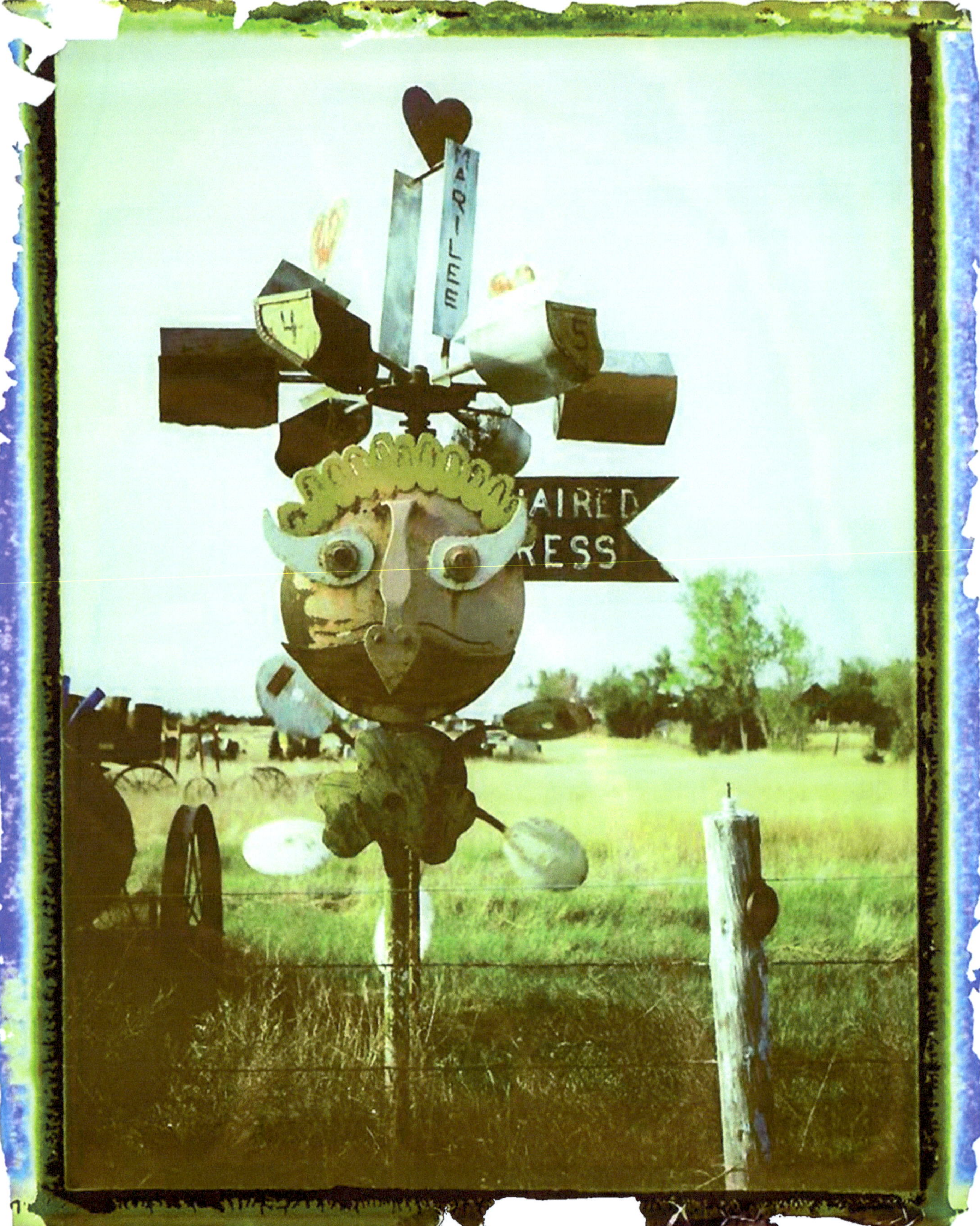

MARILEE
4
5
PRAIRIE
PRESS

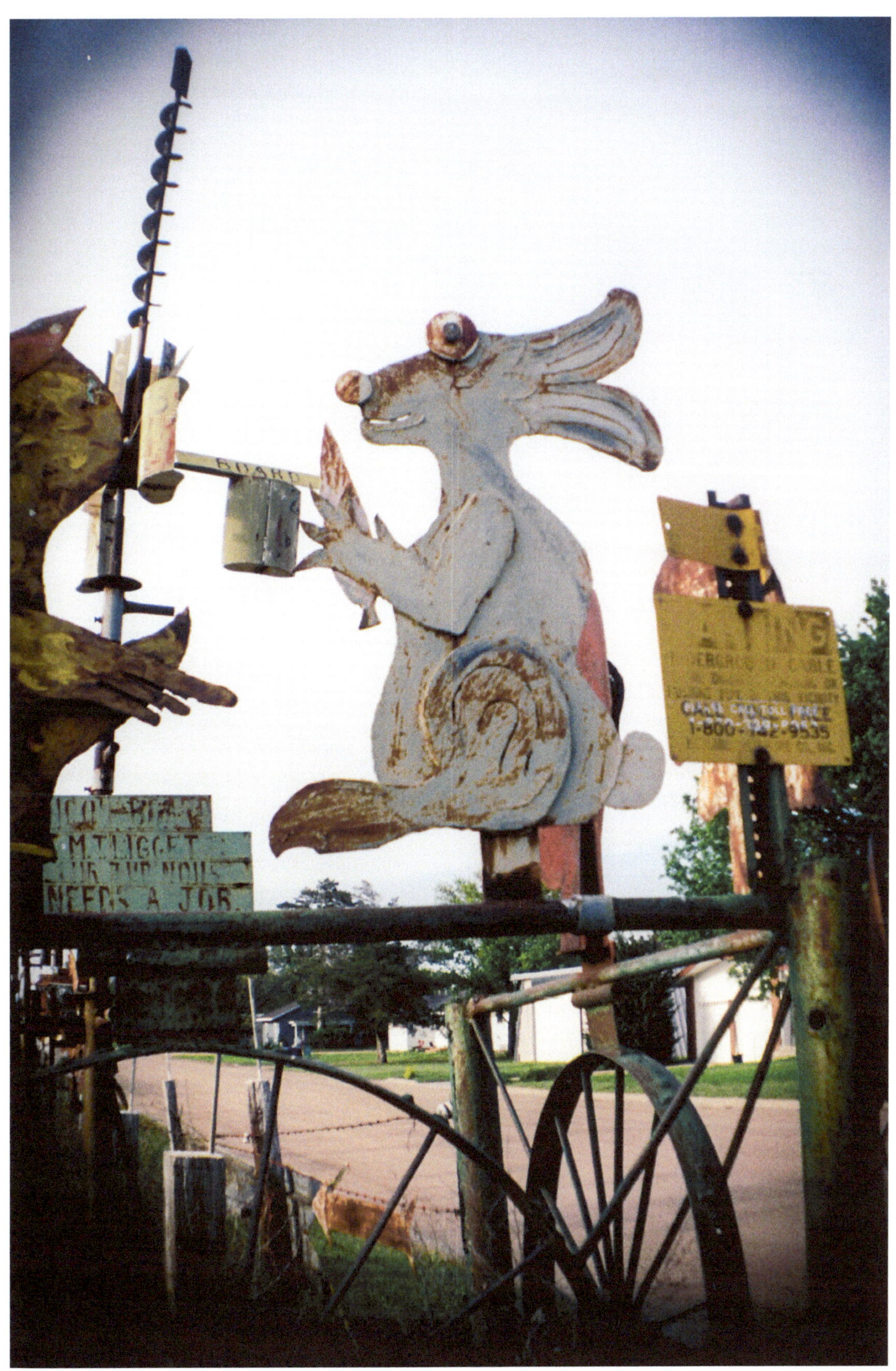

M.T. LIGGET
NEEDS A JOB.
CALL US TOLL FREE
1-800-742-9535

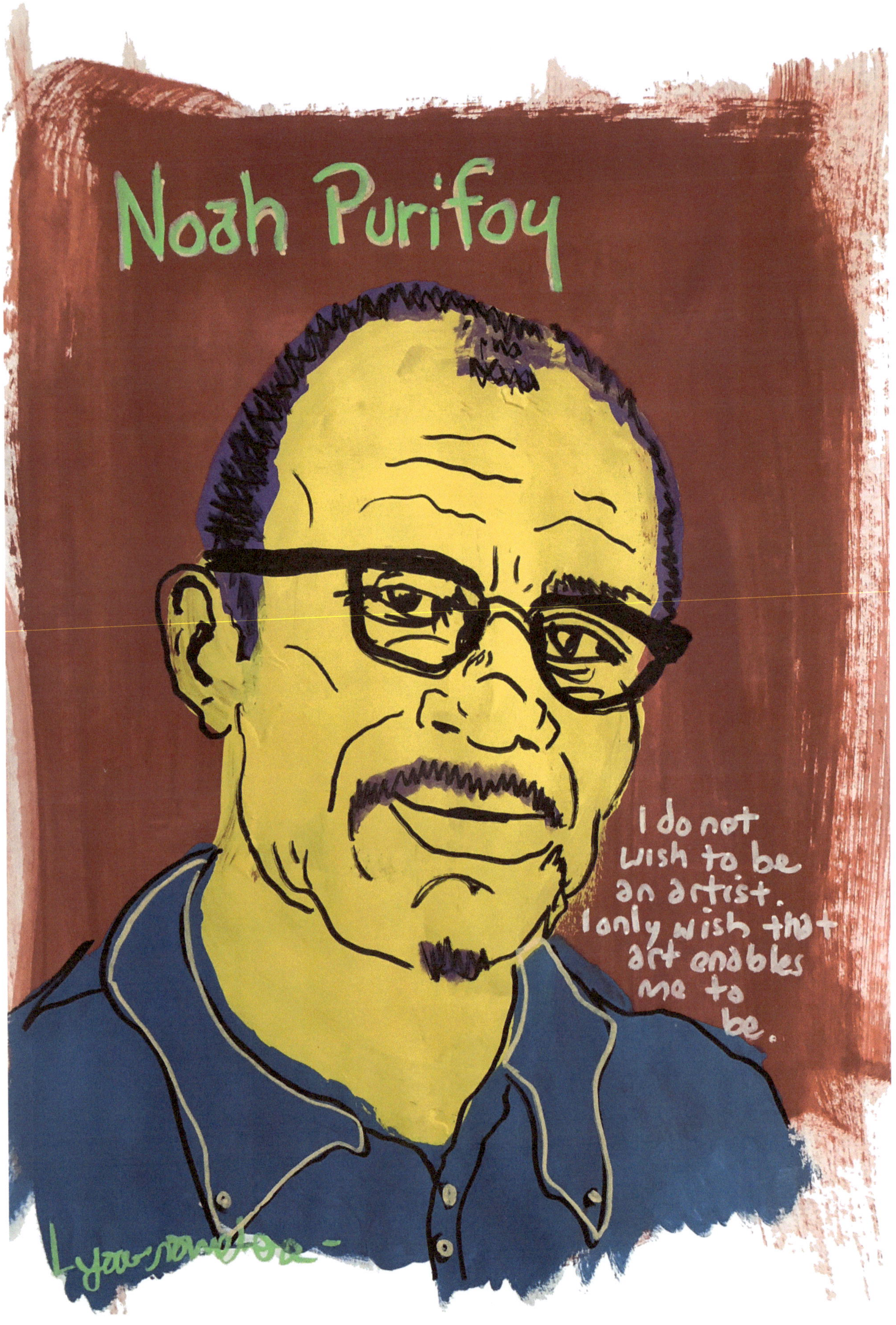

Noah Purifoy
I do not
wish to be
an artist.
I only wish that
art enables
me to
be.

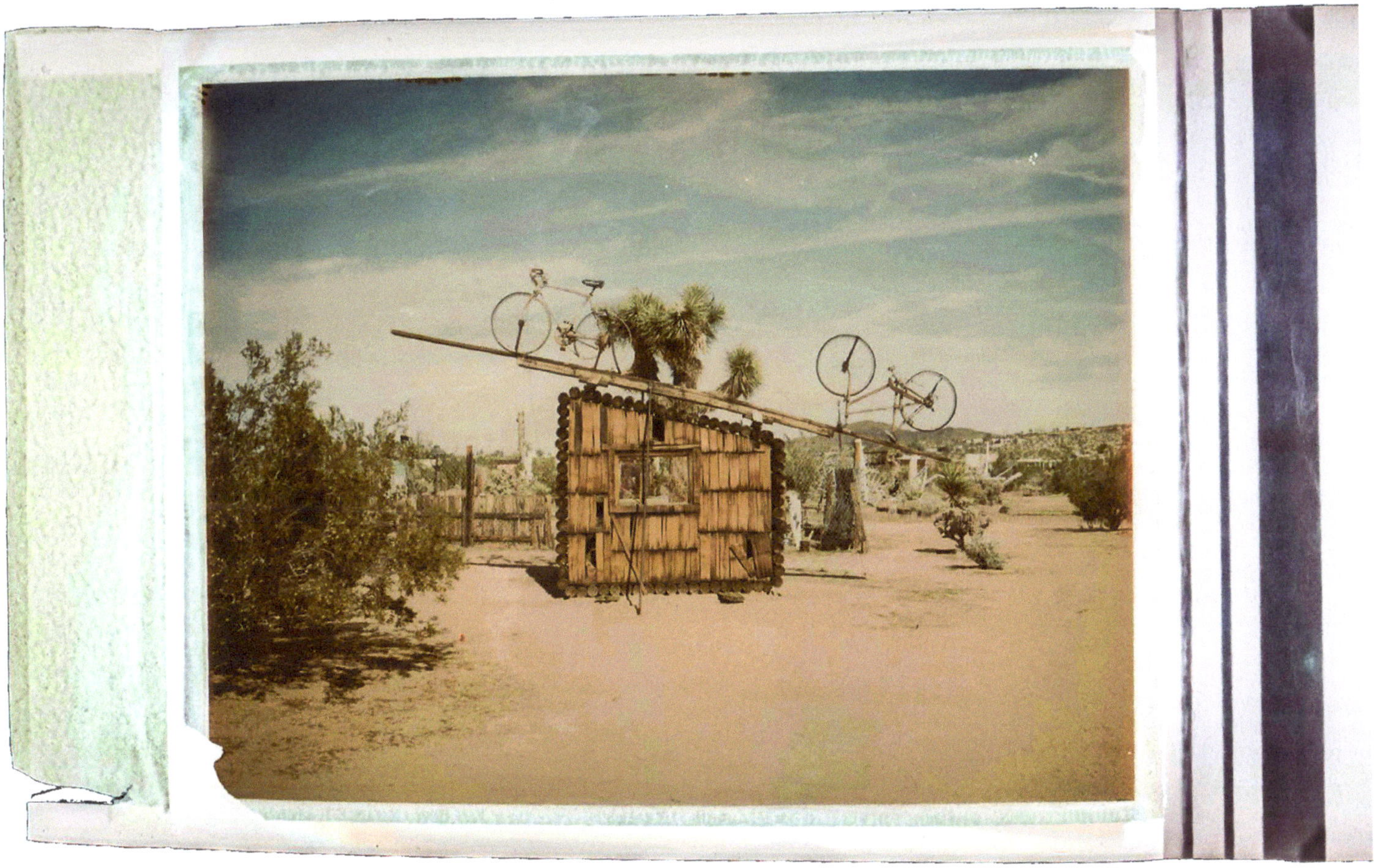

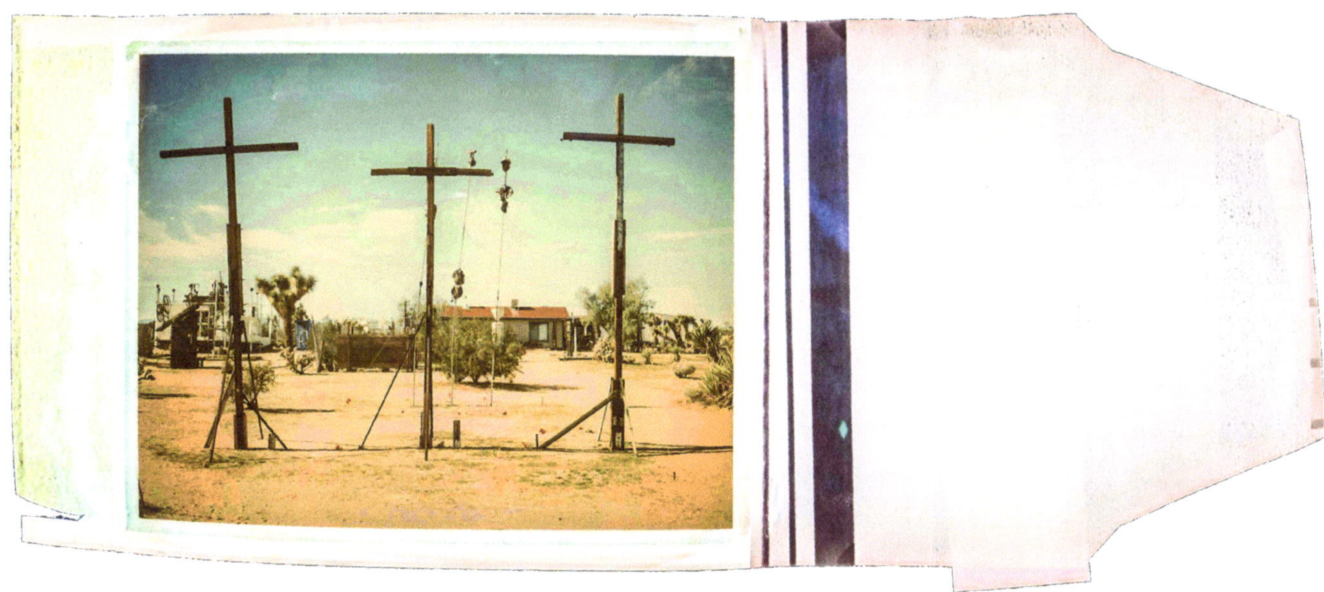

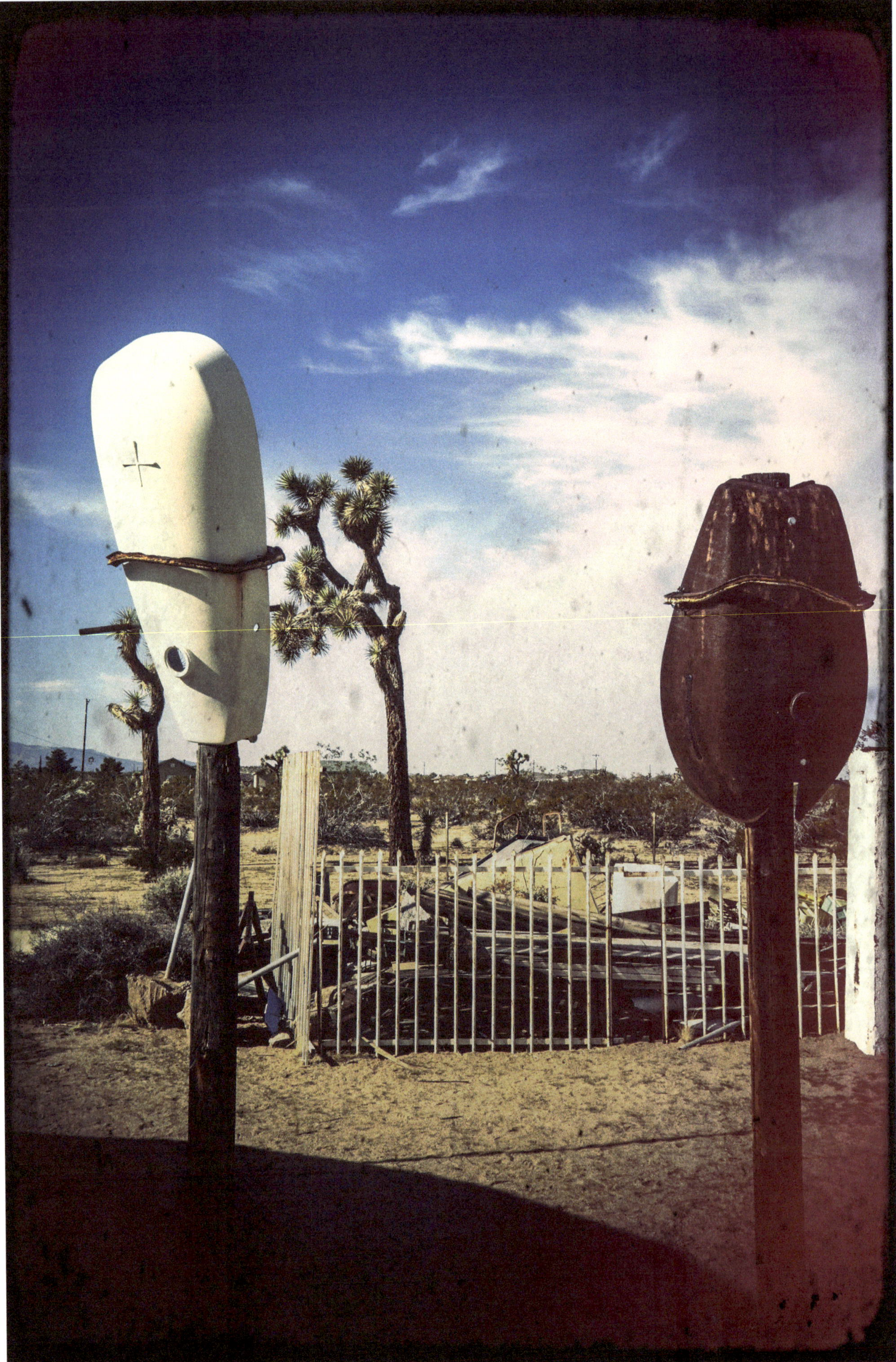

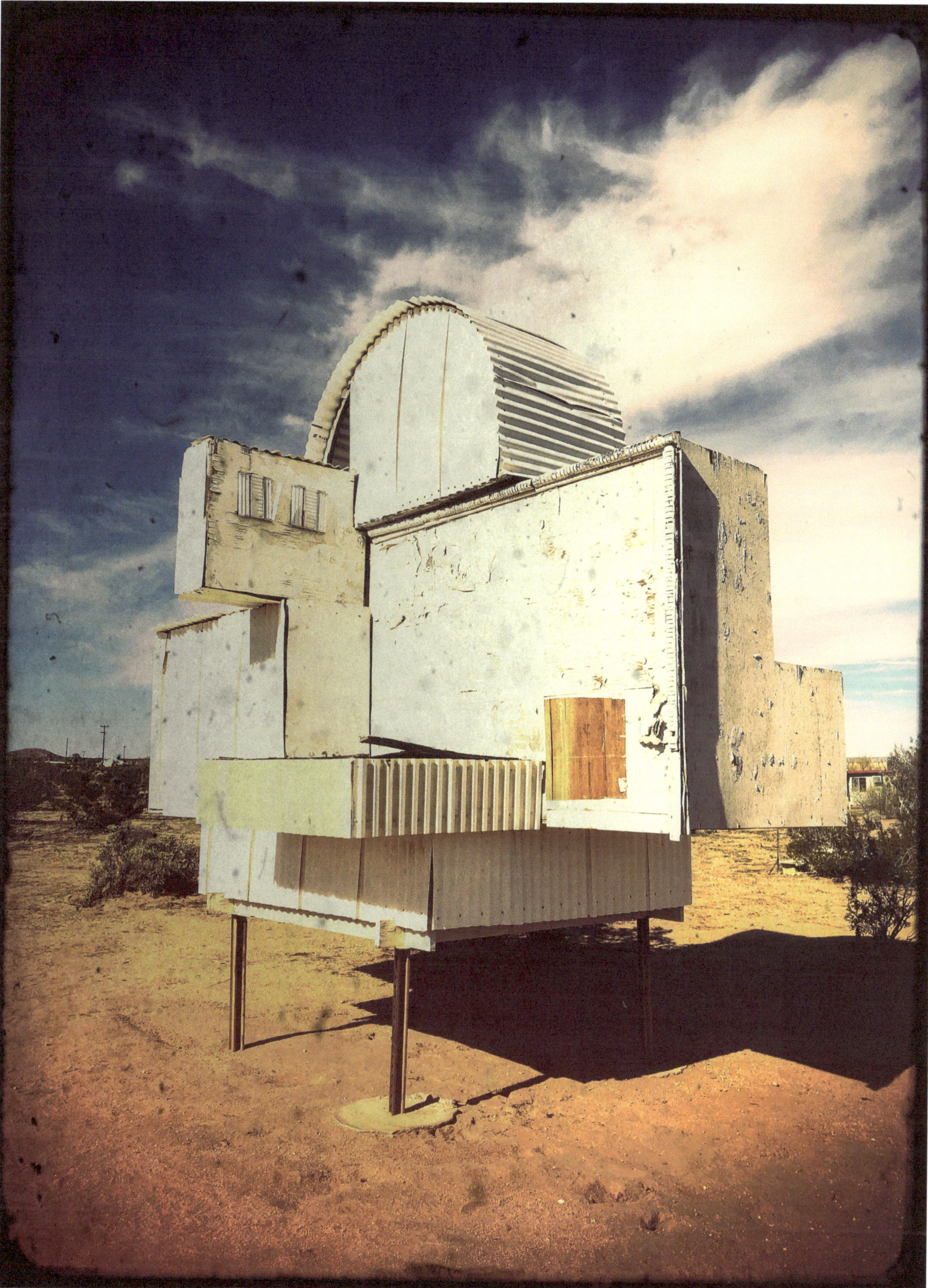

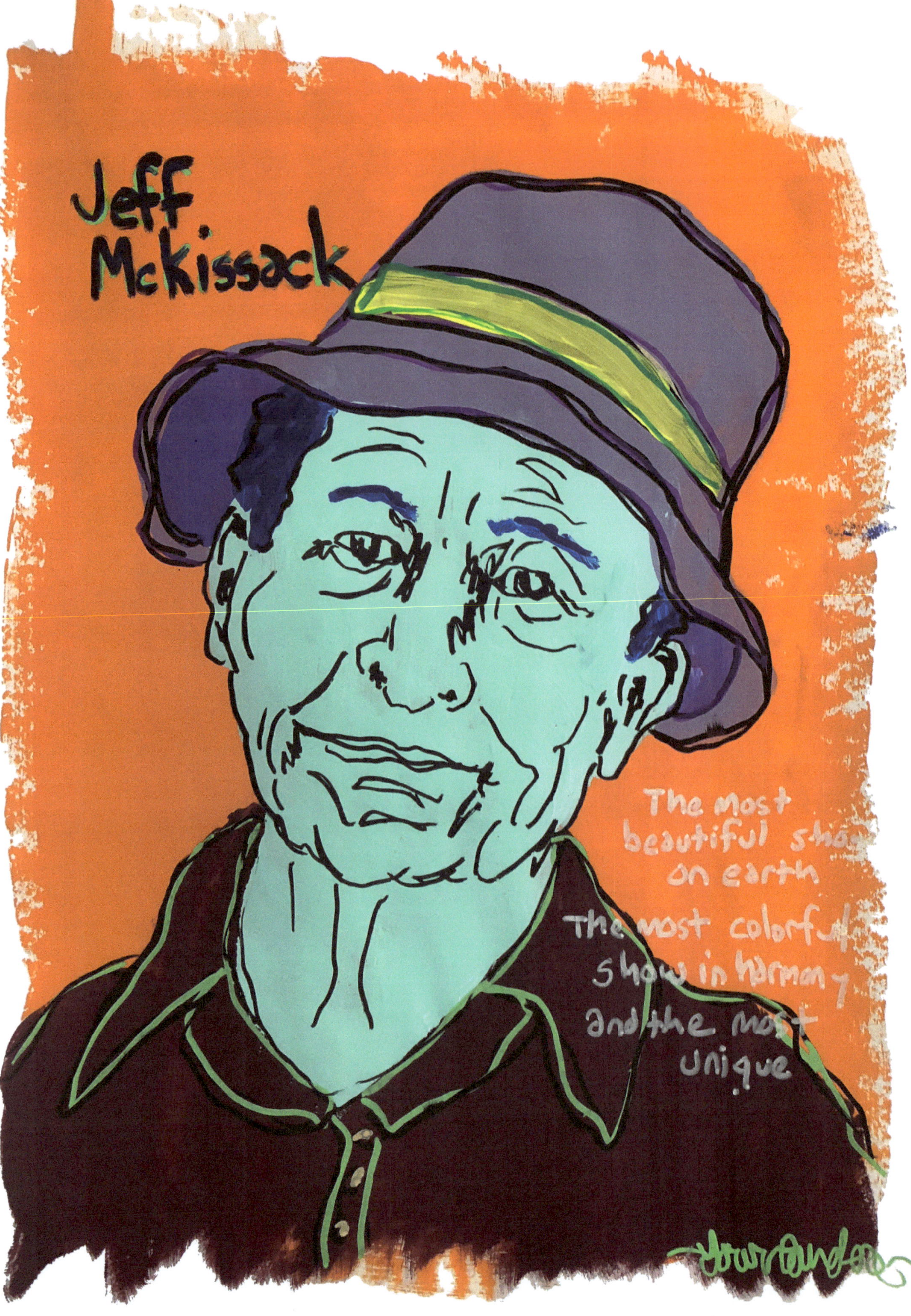

Jeff.
McKissack
The most
beautiful show
on earth
The most colorful
show in harmony
and the most
unique

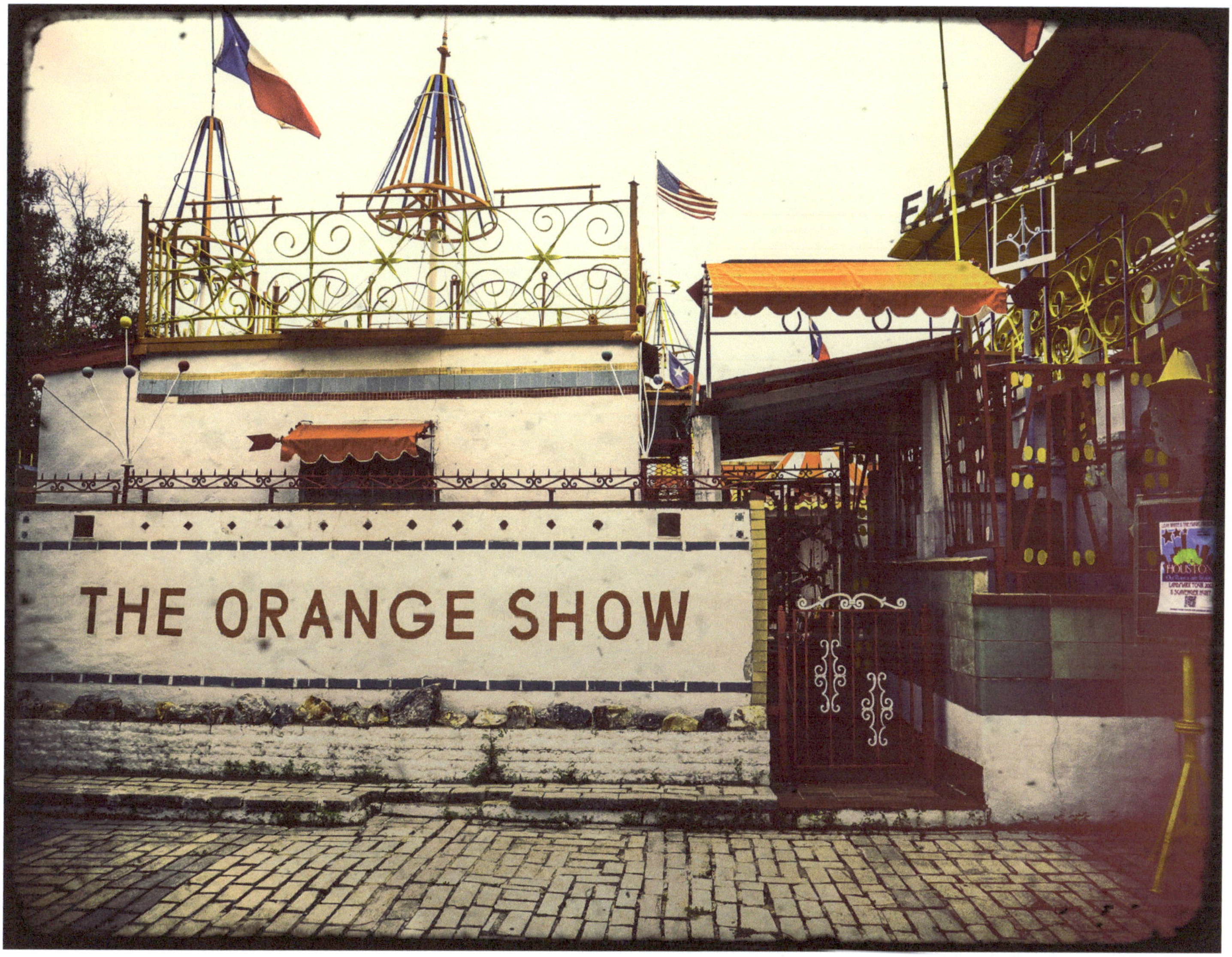

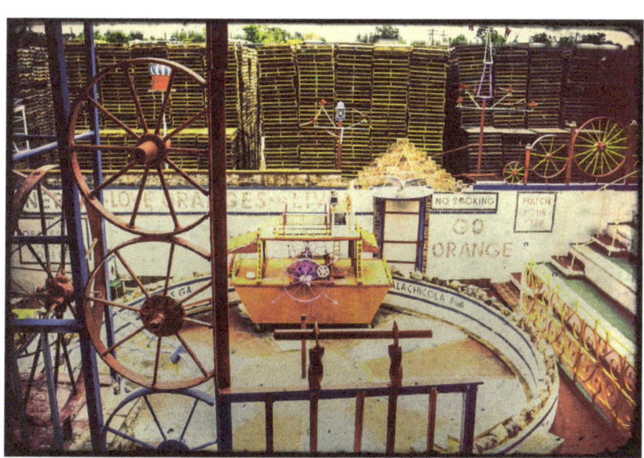

NO SMOKING
WATCH YOUR STEP
GO ORANGE
APALACHICOLA Fla

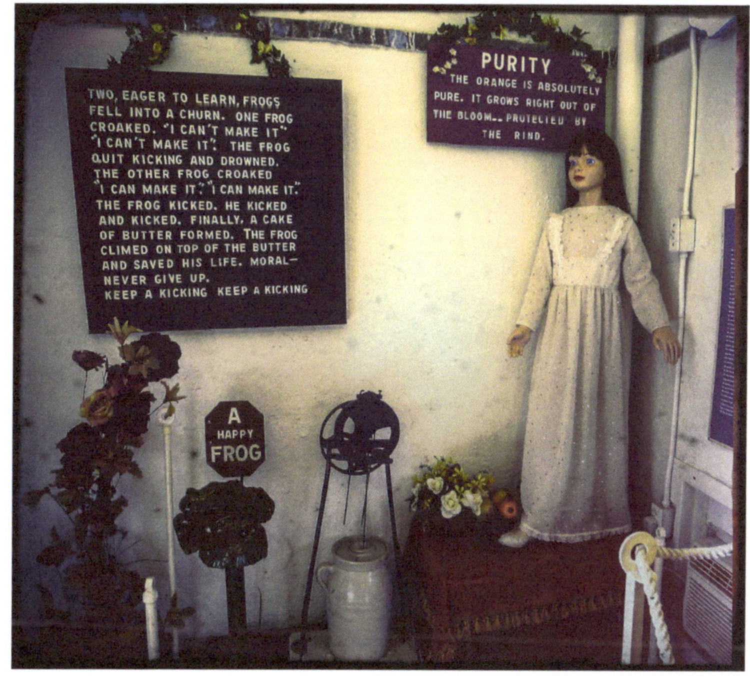

TWO, EAGER TO LEARN, FROGS
FELL INTO A CHURN. ONE FROG
CROAKED. "I CAN'T MAKE IT"
"I CAN'T MAKE IT". THE FROG
QUIT KICKING AND DROWNED.
THE OTHER FROG CROAKED
"I CAN MAKE IT." "I CAN MAKE IT".
THE FROG KICKED. HE KICKED
AND KICKED. FINALLY, A CAKE
OF BUTTER FORMED. THE FROG
CLIMED ON TOP OF THE BUTTER
AND SAVED HIS LIFE. MORAL—
NEVER GIVE UP.
KEEP A KICKING KEEP A KICKING
PURITY
THE ORANGE IS ABSOLUTELY
PURE. IT GROWS RIGHT OUT OF
THE BLOOM...PROTECTED BY
THE RIND.
A HAPPY FROG

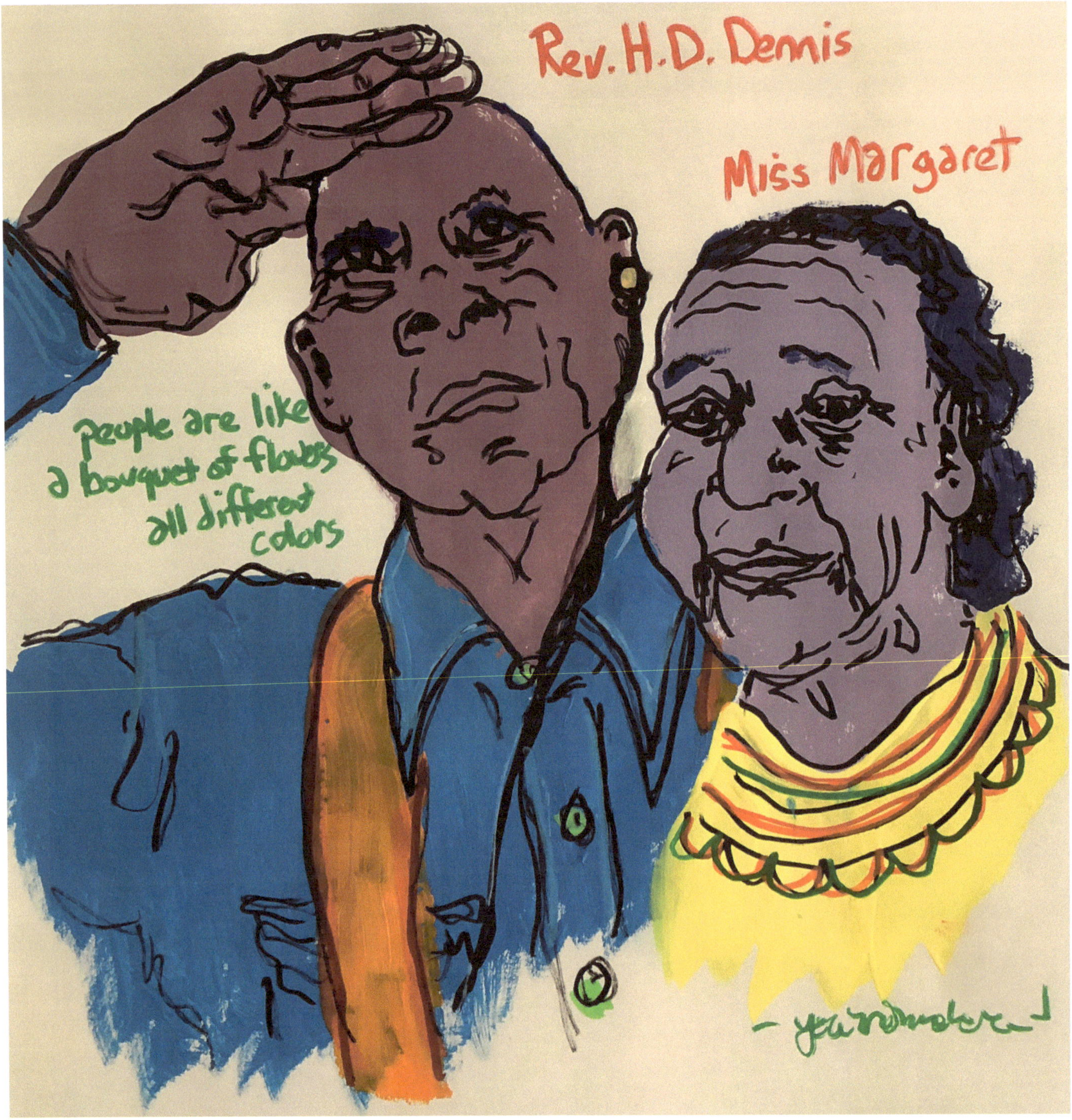

Rev. H.D. Dennis

Miss Margaret

people are like
a bouquet of flowers
all different
colors

— yando dotered

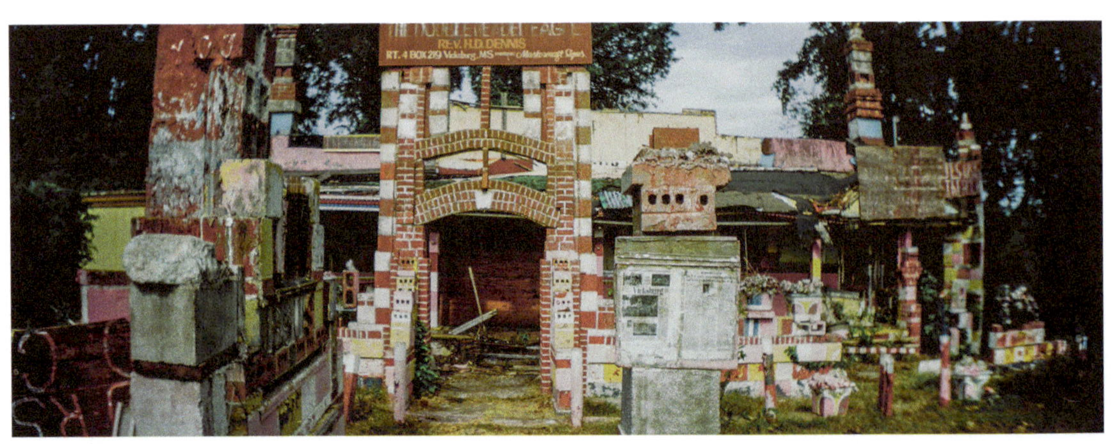

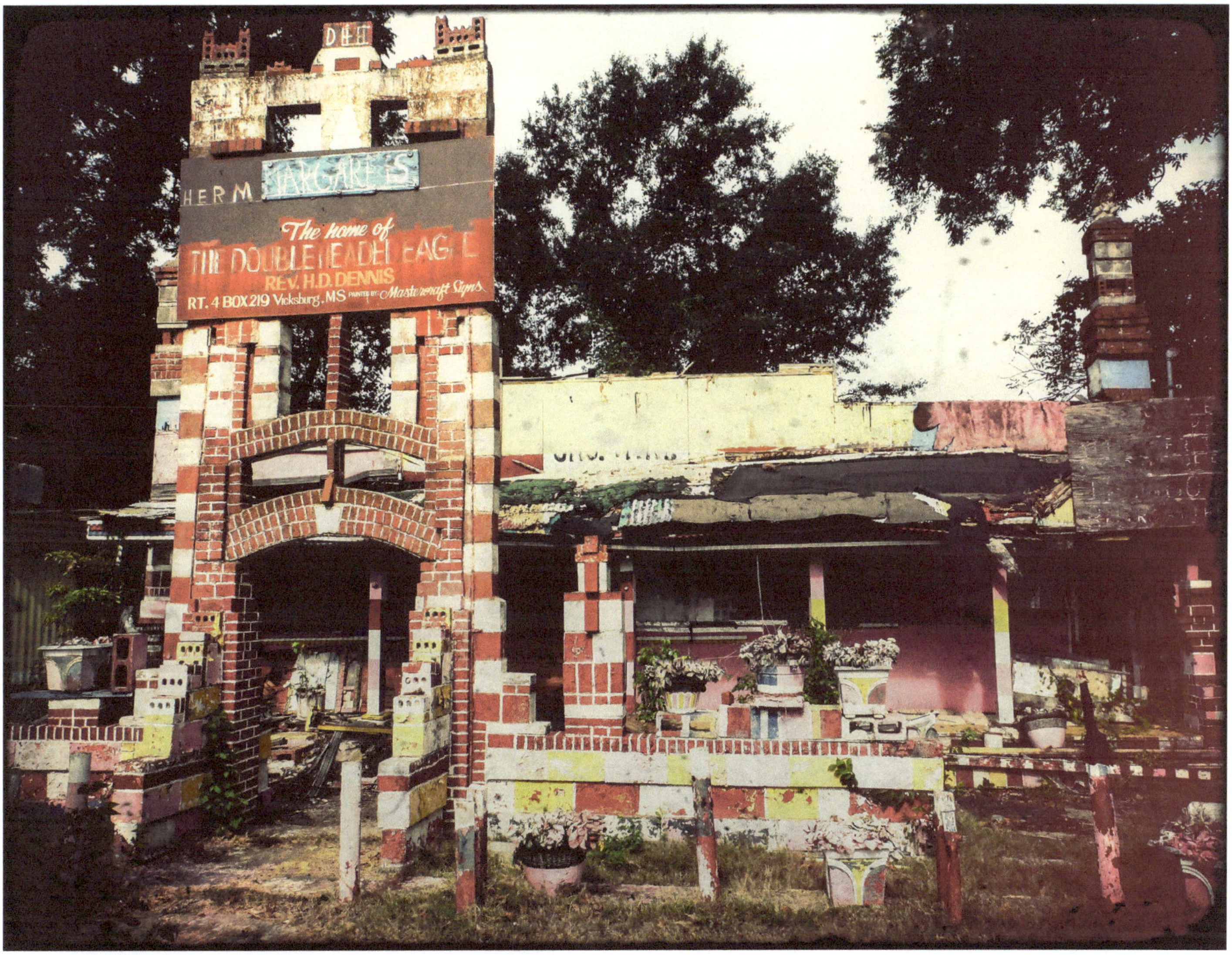

HERM
BARGAINS
The home of
THE DOUBLE HEADED EAGLE
REV. H.D. DENNIS
RT. 4 BOX 219 Vicksburg, MS PAINTED BY Mastercraft Signs

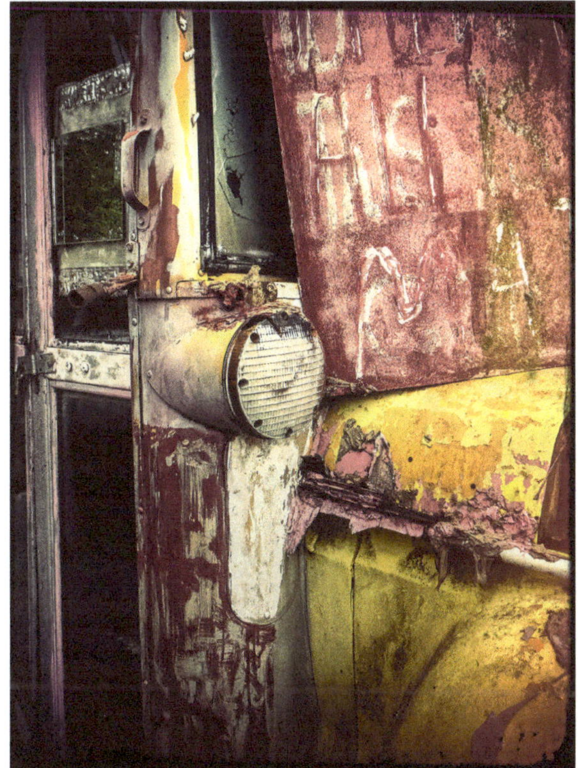

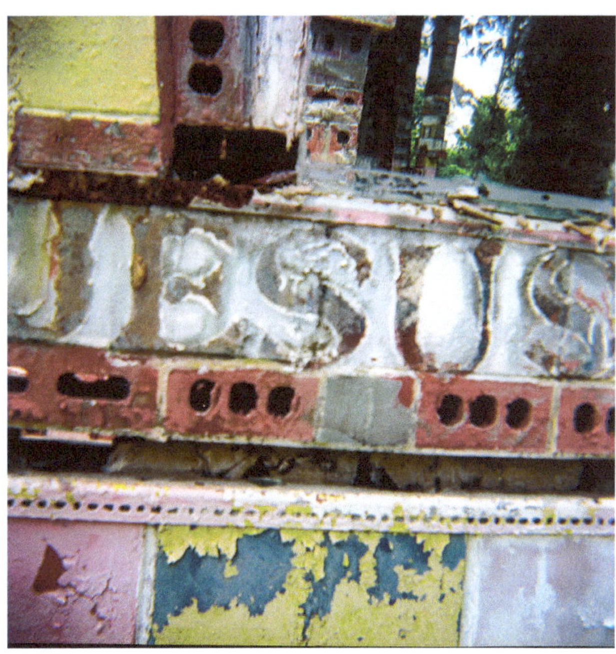
JESUS

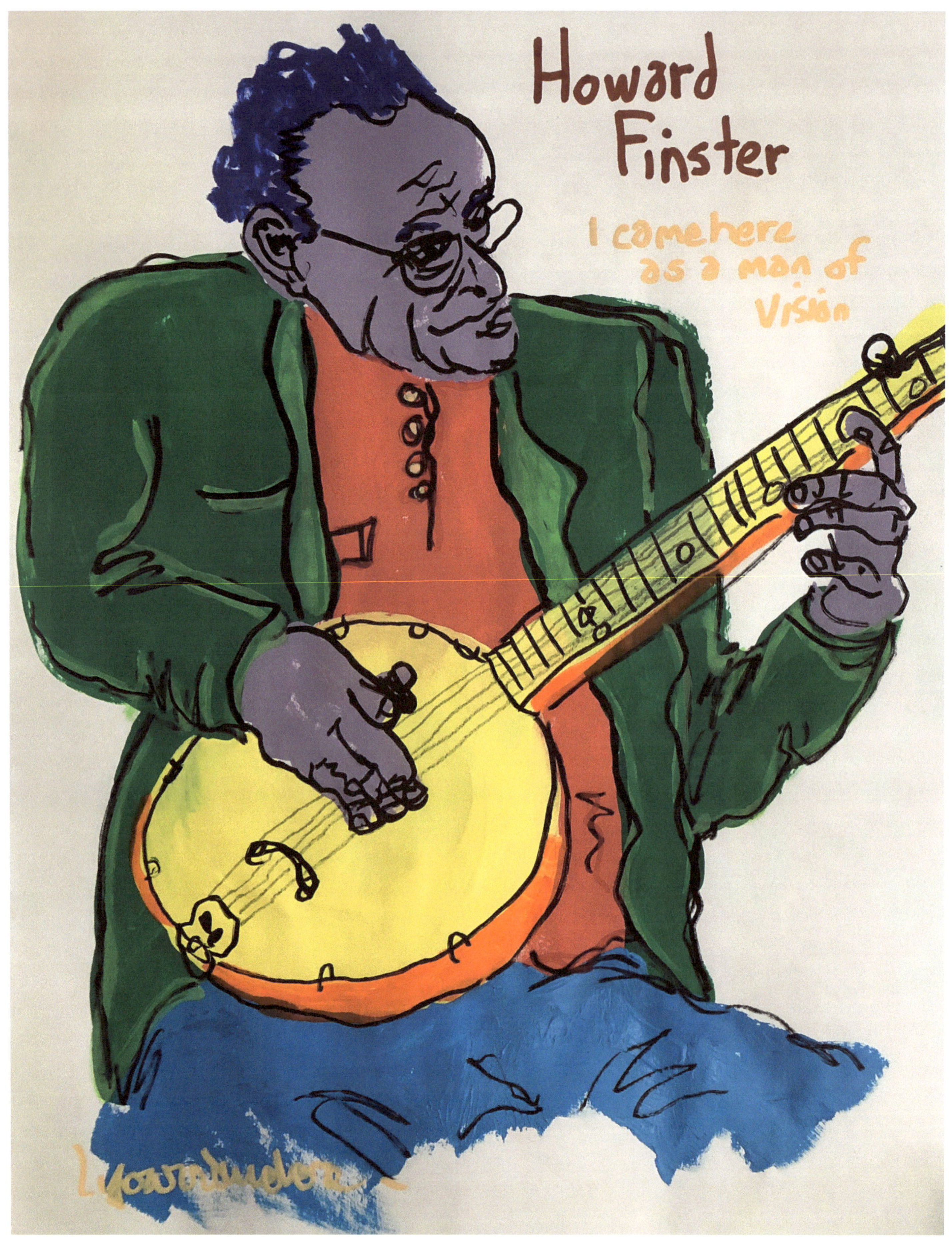

Howard
Finster
I came here
as a man of
Vision

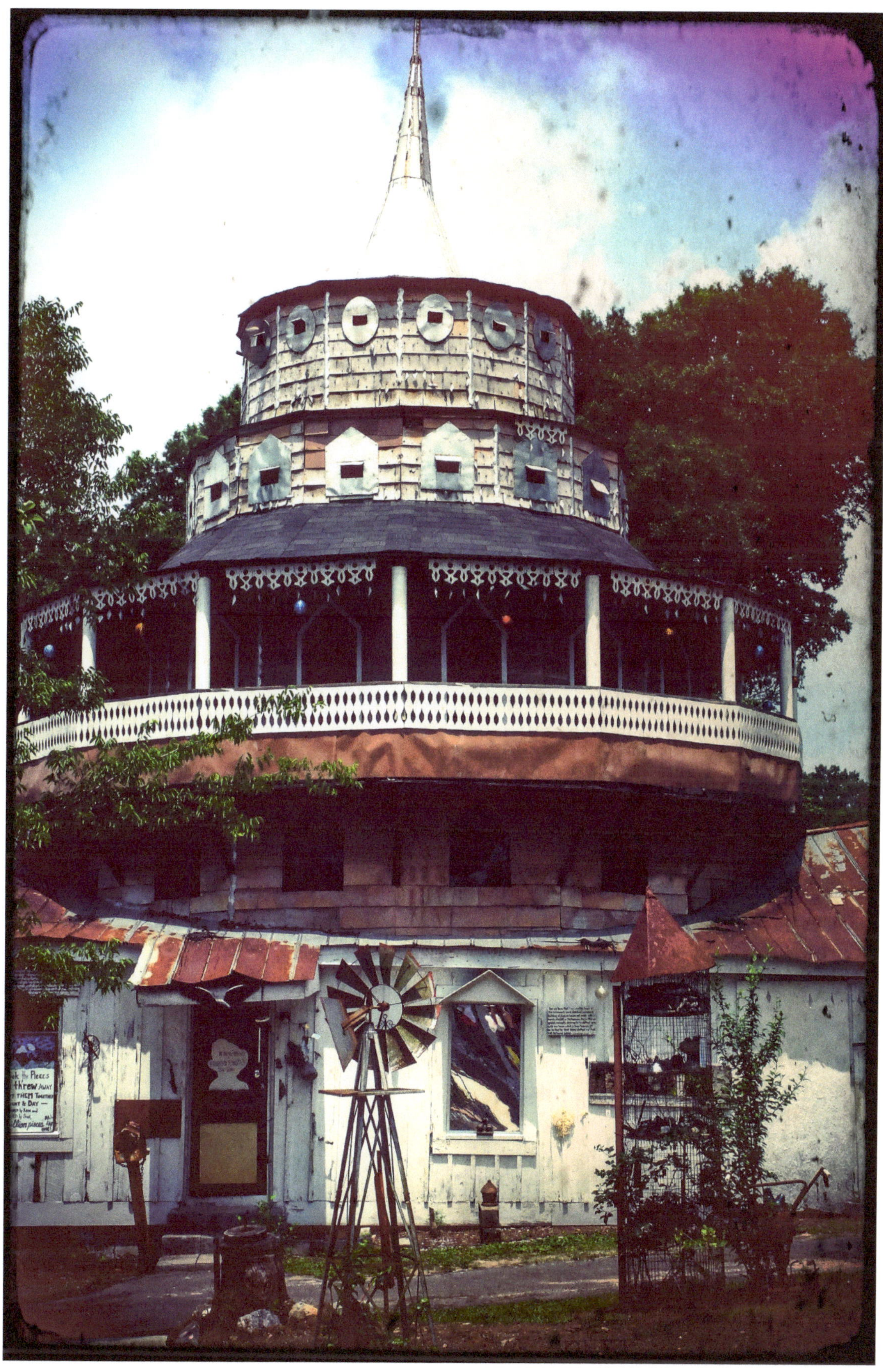

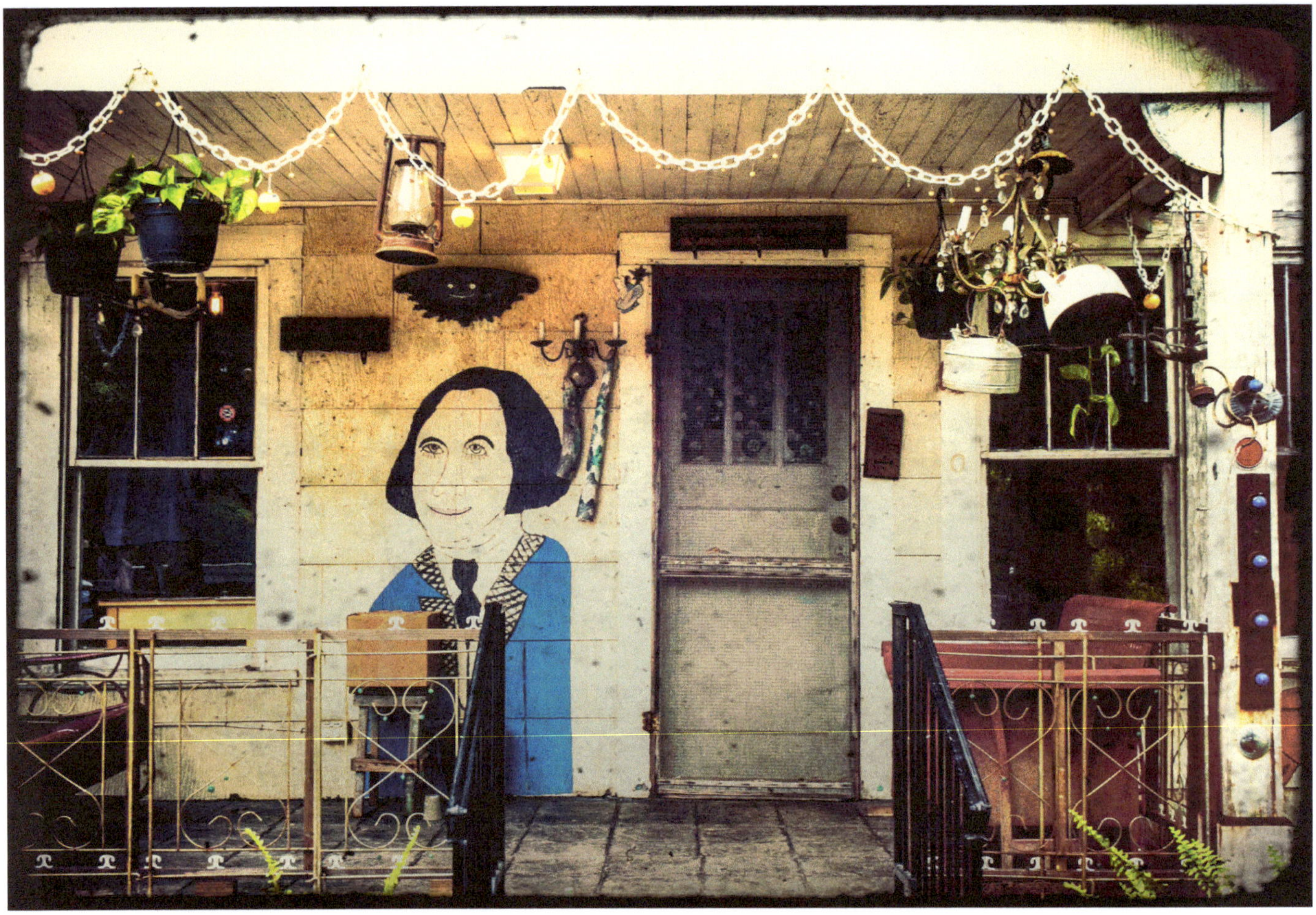

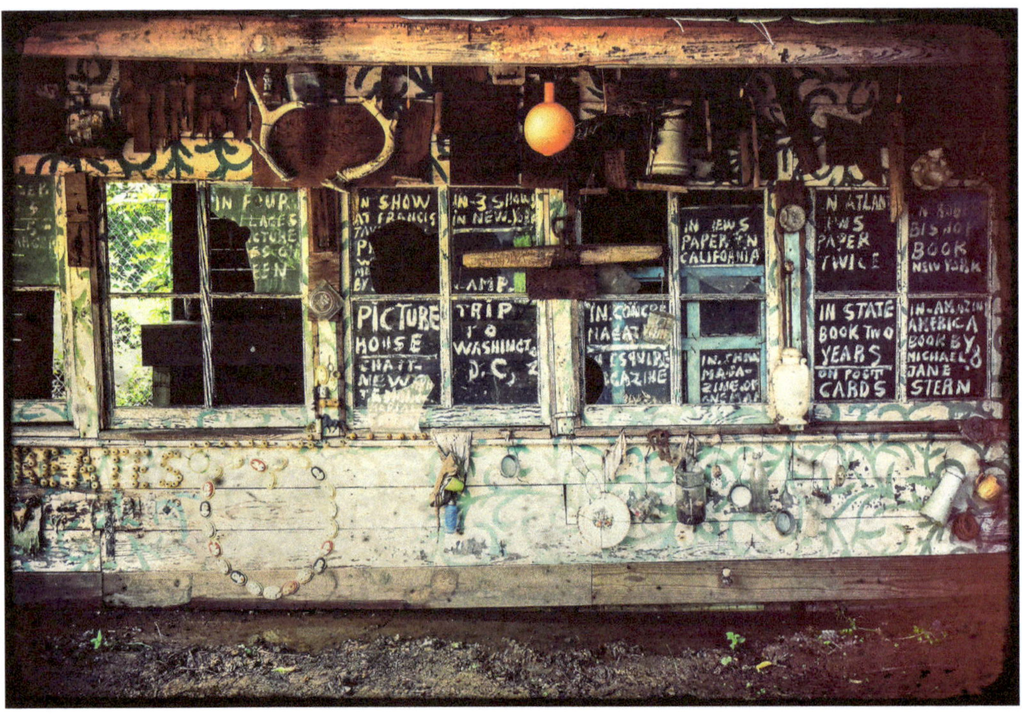

IN FOUR PLACES PICTURE ESG SCREEN
IN SHOW AT FRANCIS TAV
PICTURE HOUSE CHATT NEW TENN
IN 3 SHOWS IN NEW YORK
LAMP
TRIP TO WASHINGT D.C.
IN CONCORD MASS ESQUIRE MAGAZINE
IN NEWS PAPER IN CALIFORNIA
IN SHOW MAGAZINE OF
IN NEWS PAPER TWICE
IN STATE BOOK TWO YEARS ON POST CARDS
IN BOOK BISHOP BOOK NEW YORK
IN AMAZING AMERICA BOOK BY MICHAEL & JANE STERN

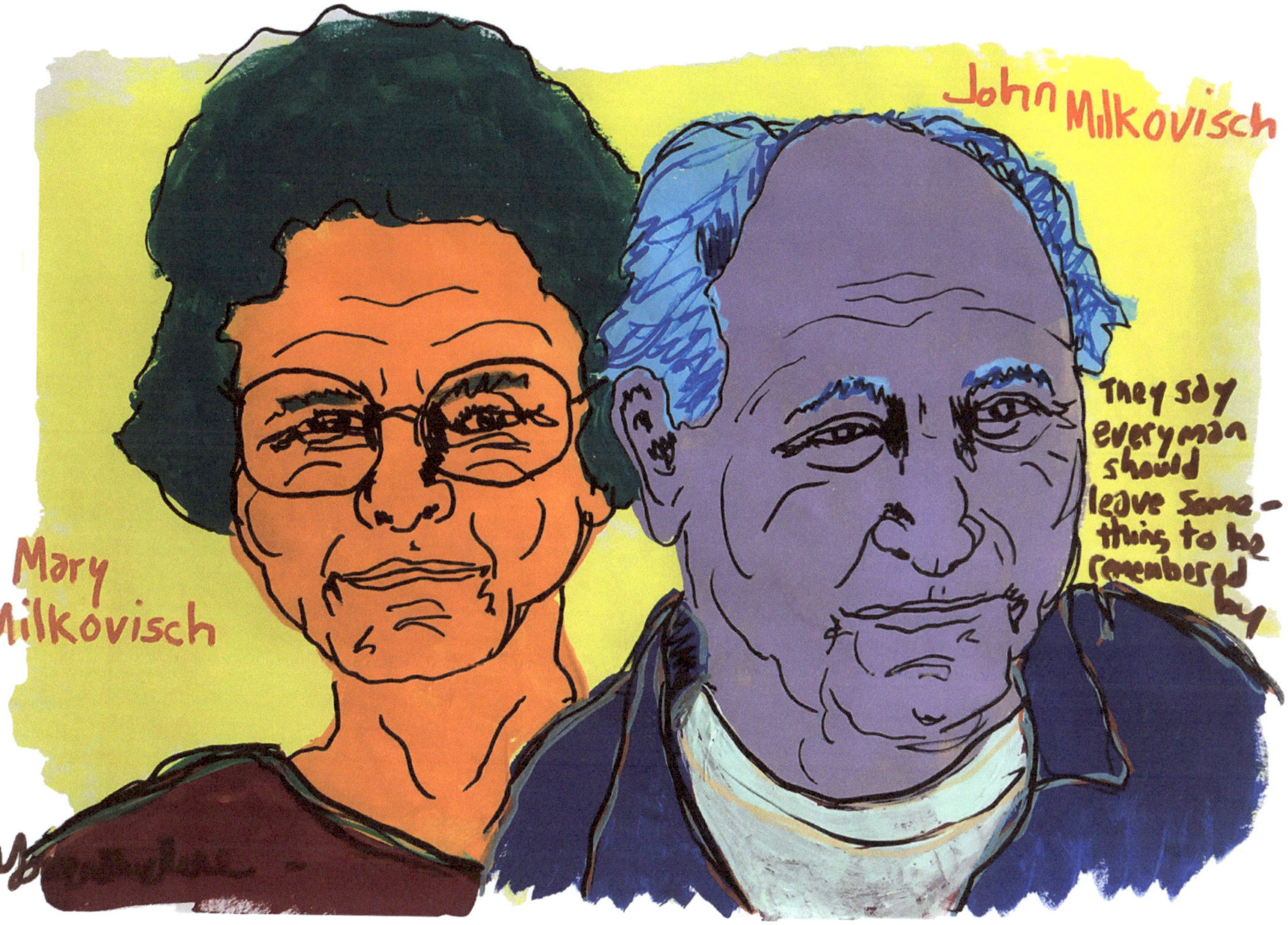

Mary
Milkovisch

John Milkovisch

They say
every man
should
leave some-
thing to be
remembered
by

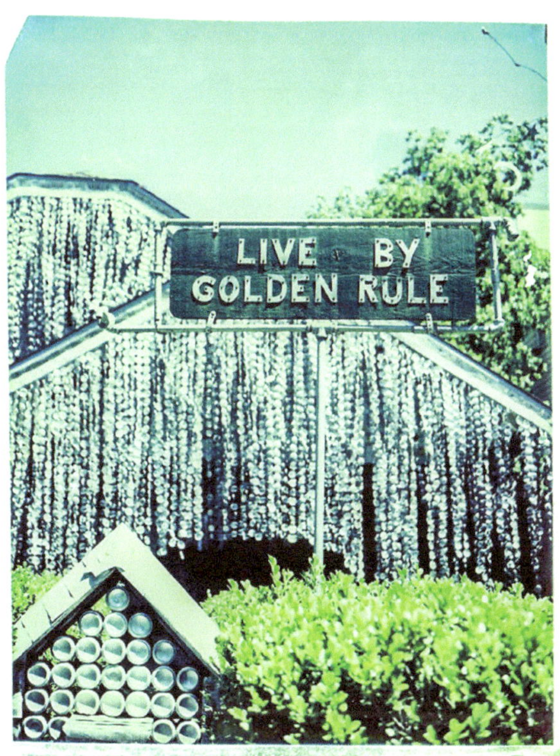

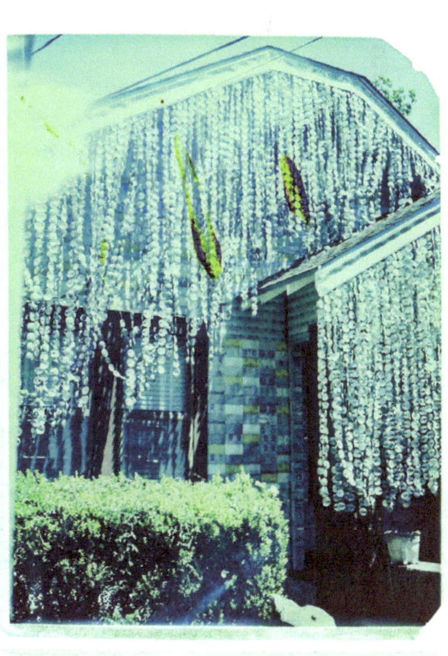

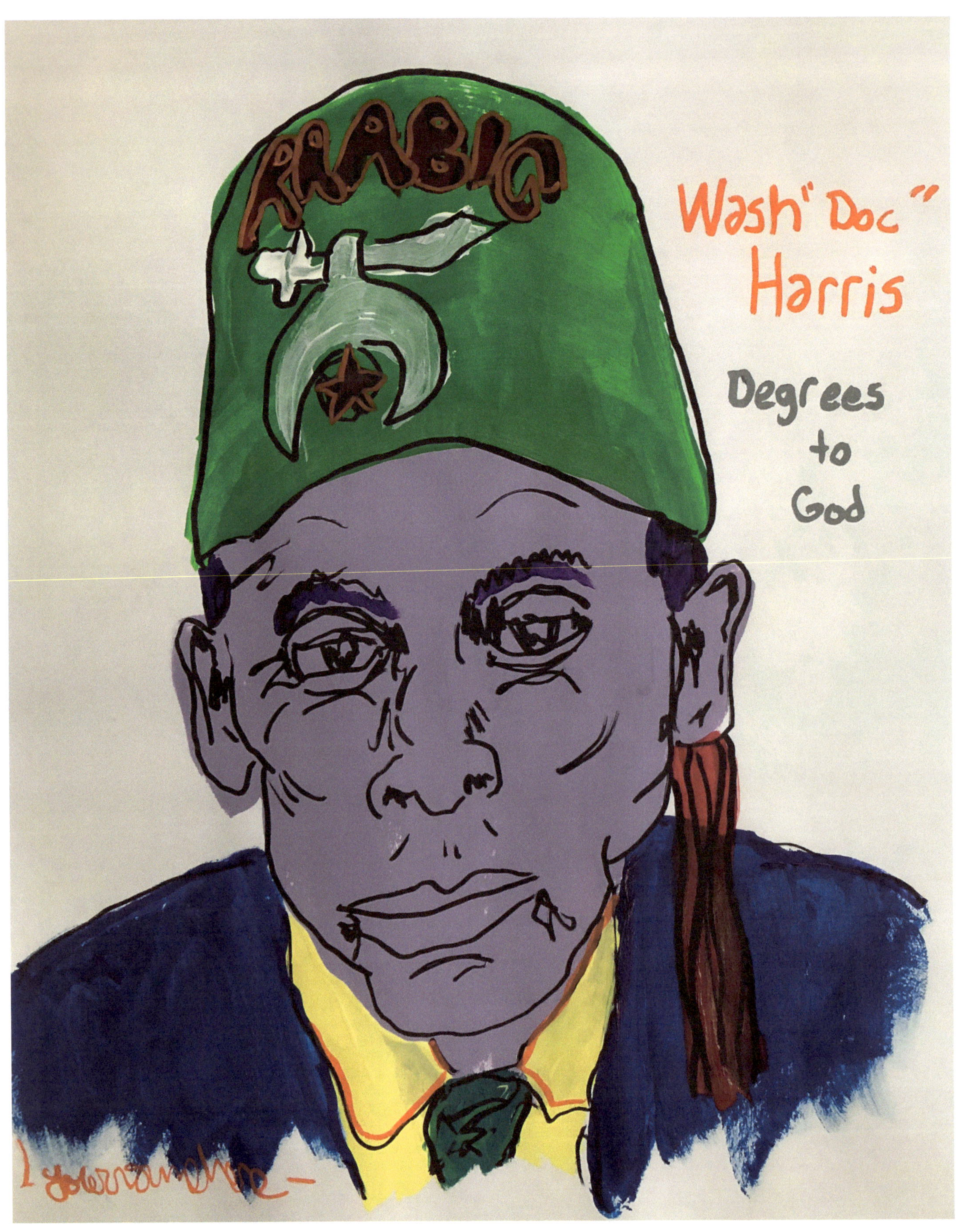
RRABIA
Wash "Doc" Harris
Degrees to God

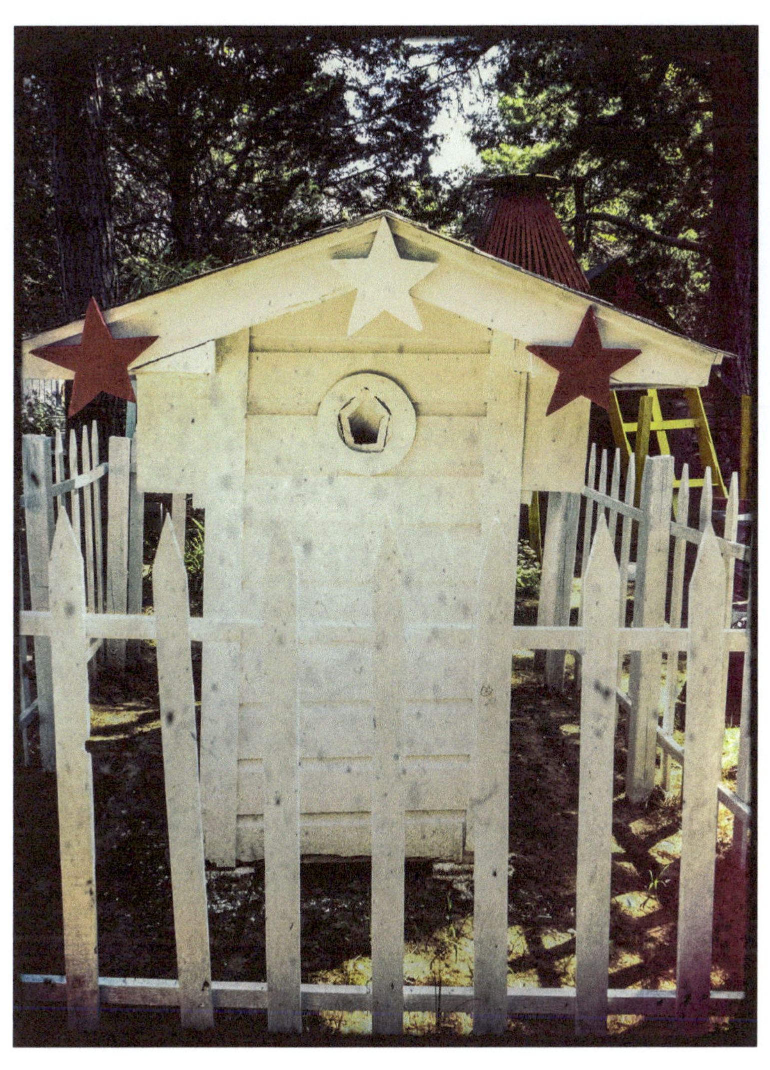

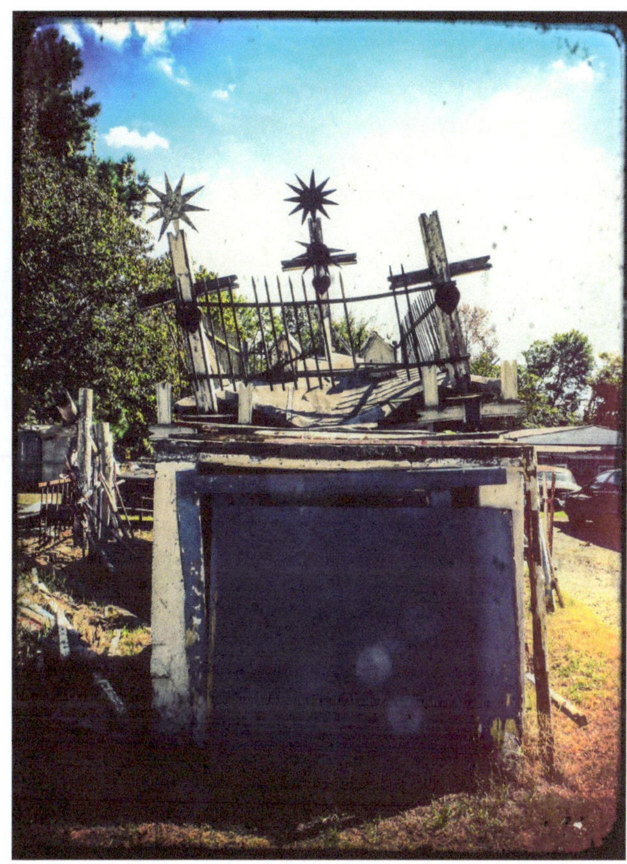

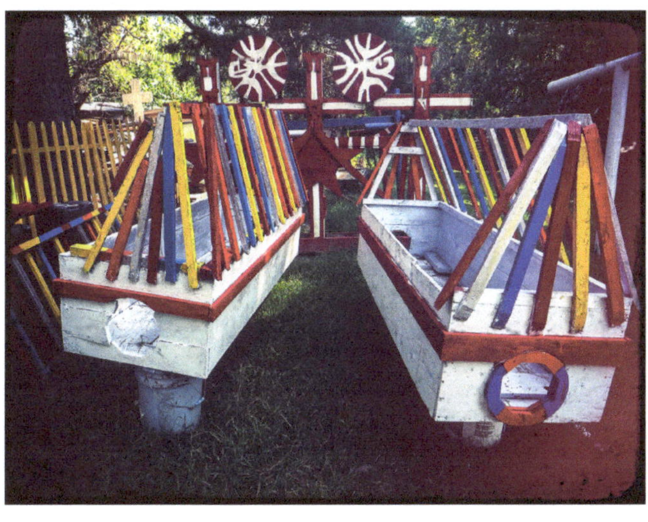

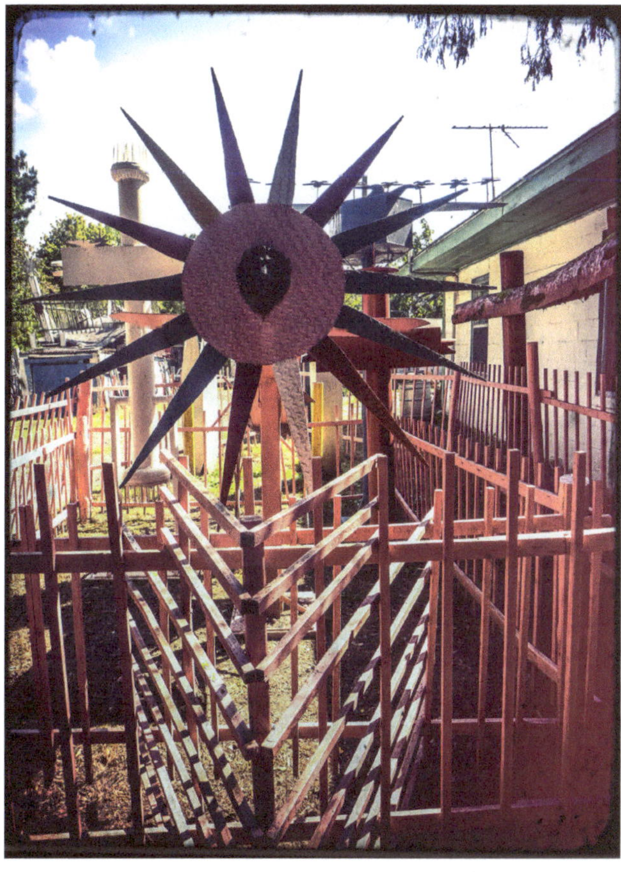

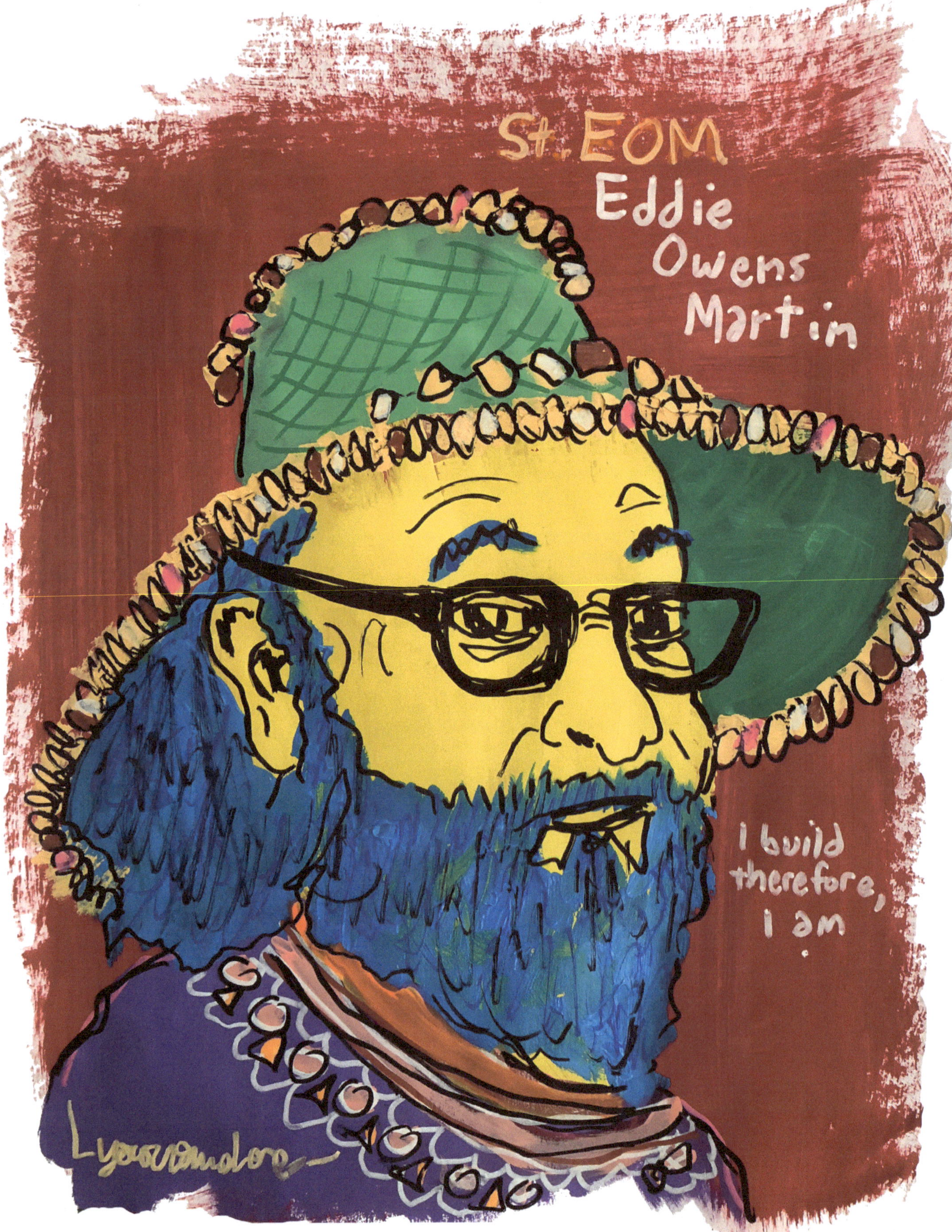
St. EOM
Eddie
Owens
Martin
I build
therefore,
I am
Lyvonadore

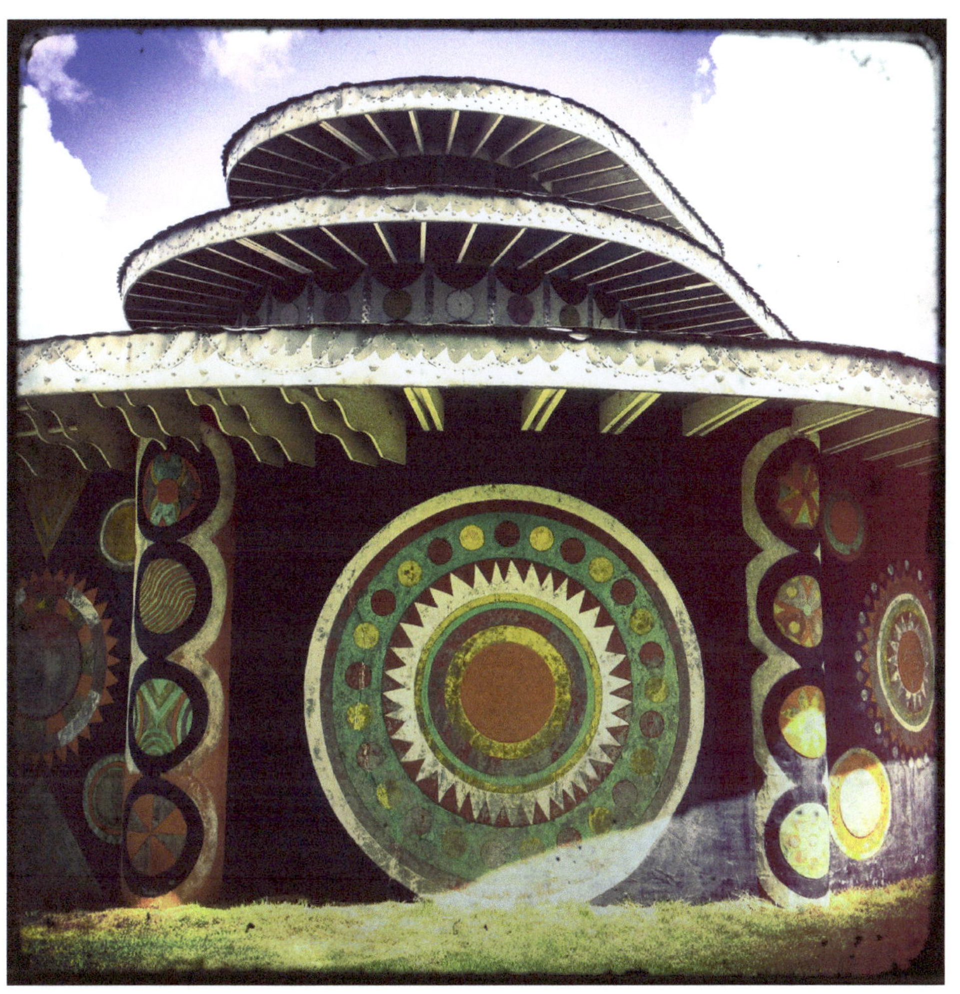
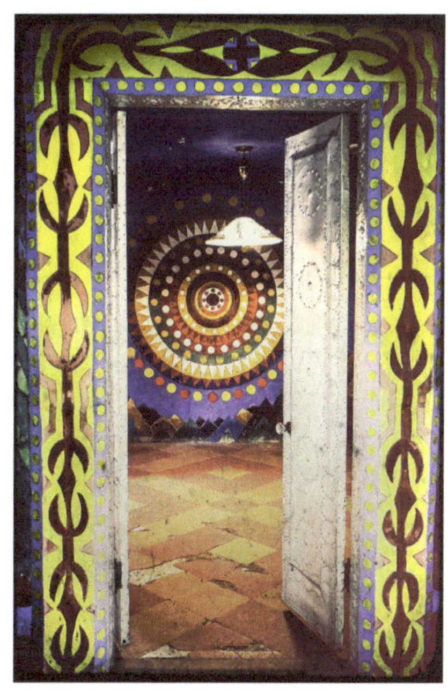
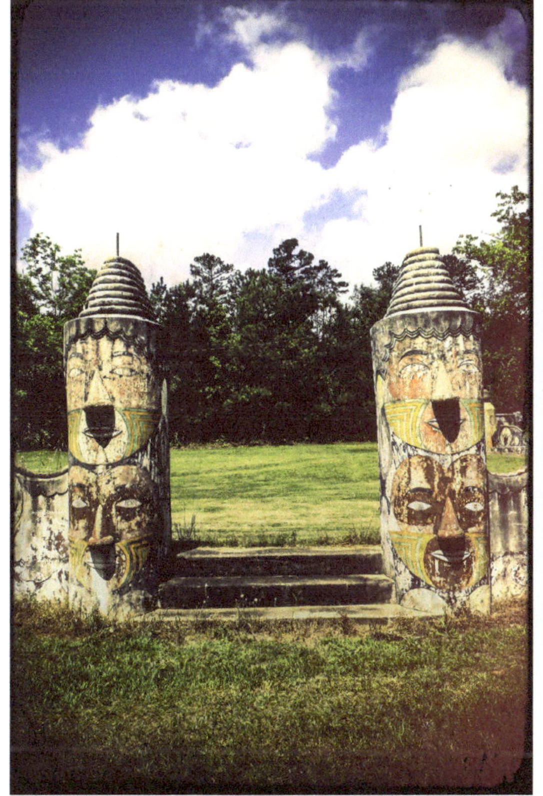
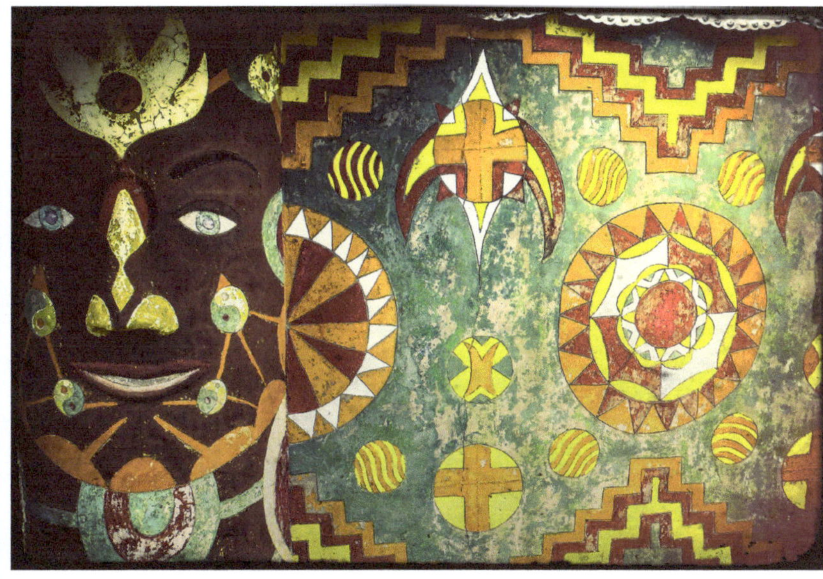

Vollis Simpson
When I got something to do, I work all day. I get tired out, I start something else

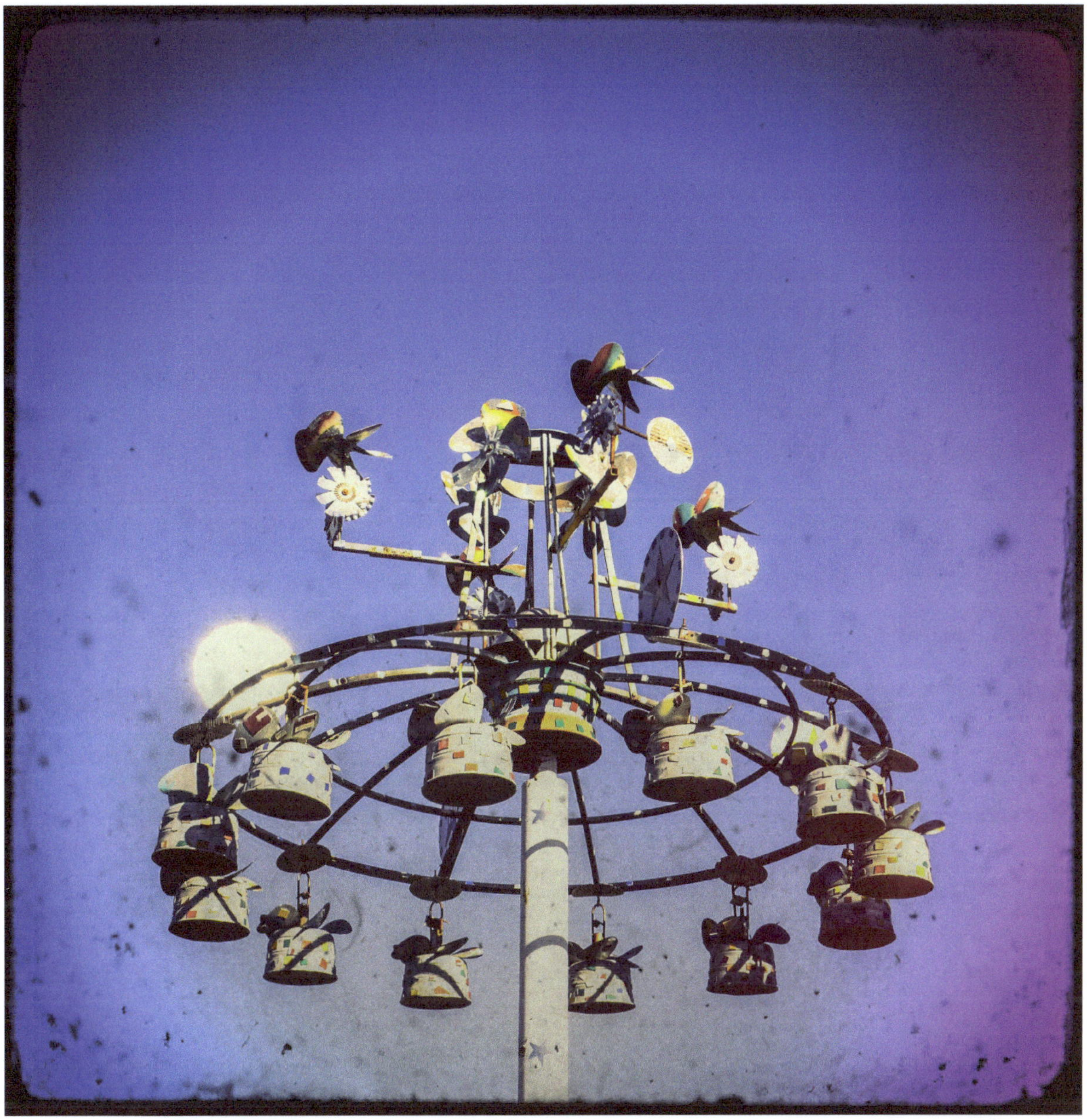

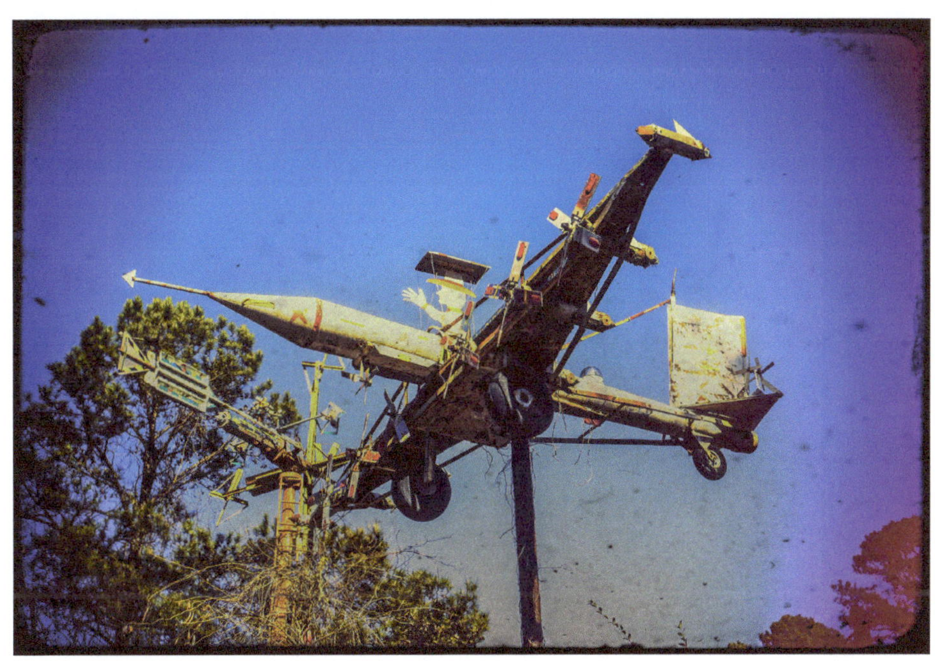

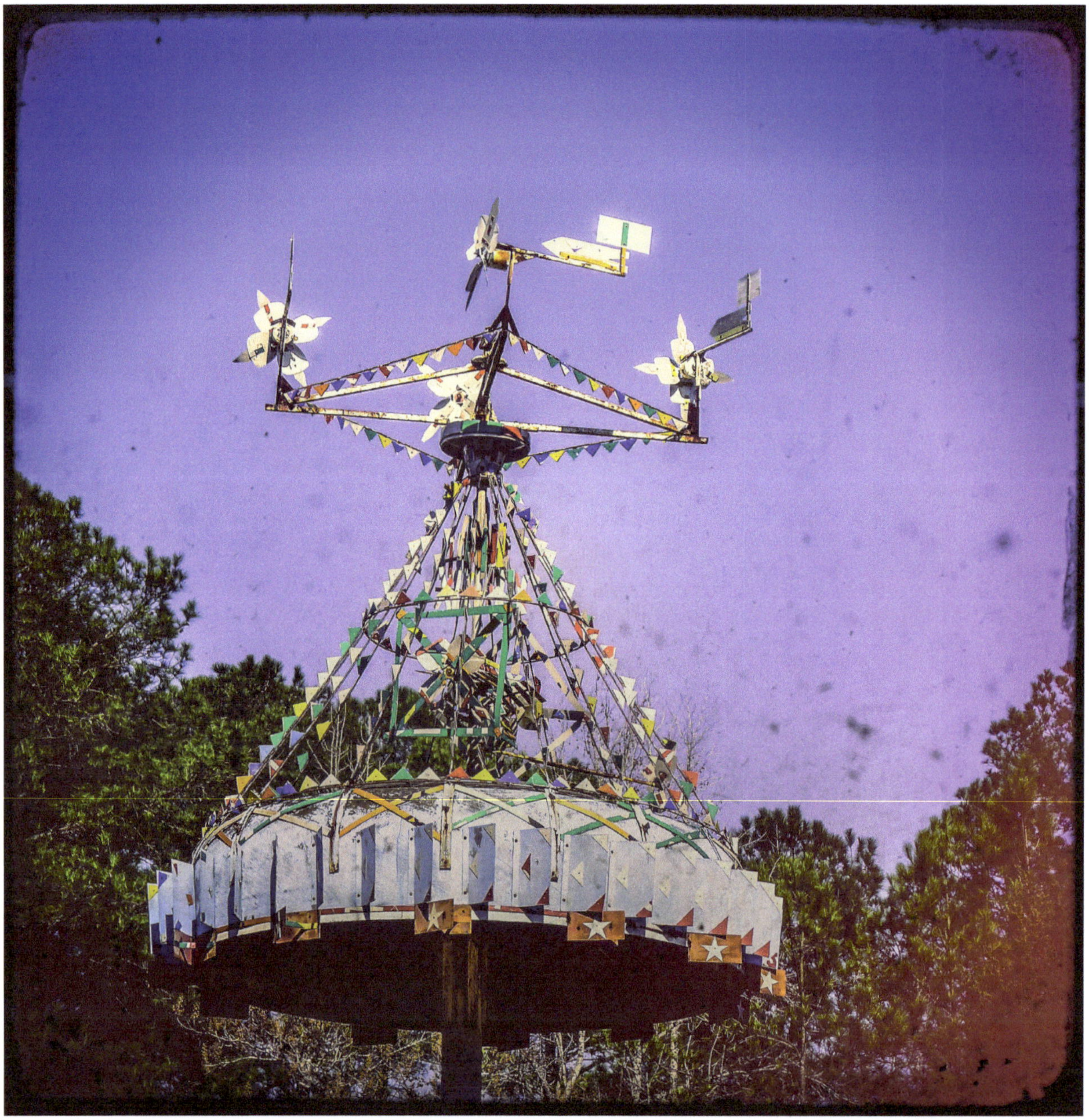

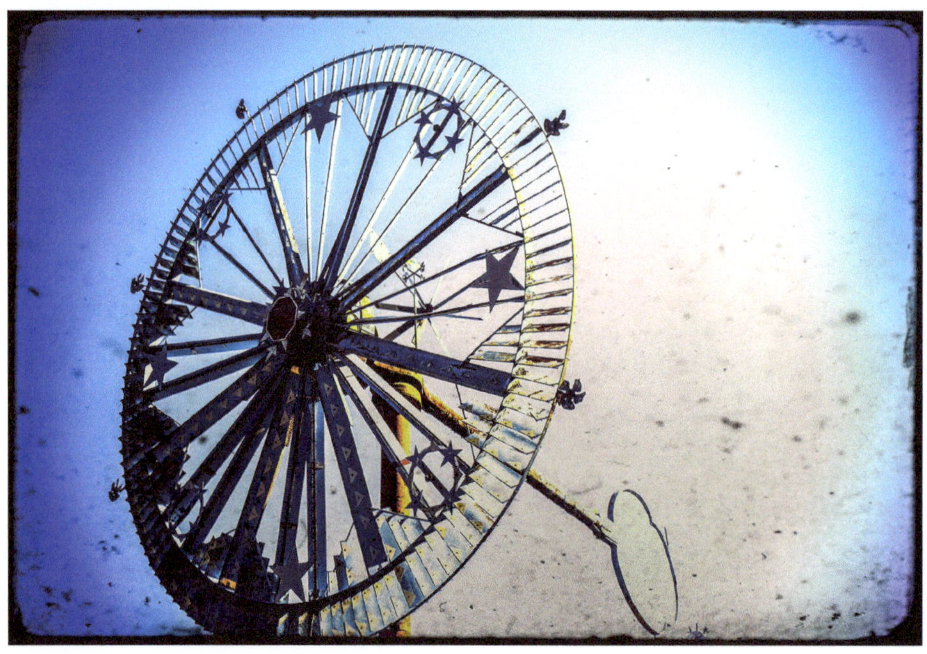

Ed Leedskalnin

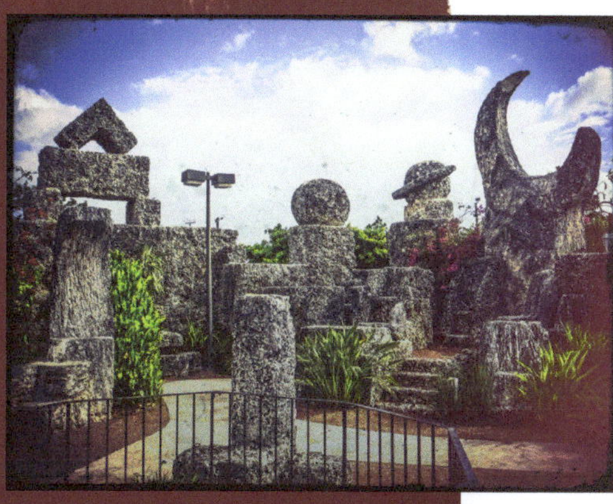

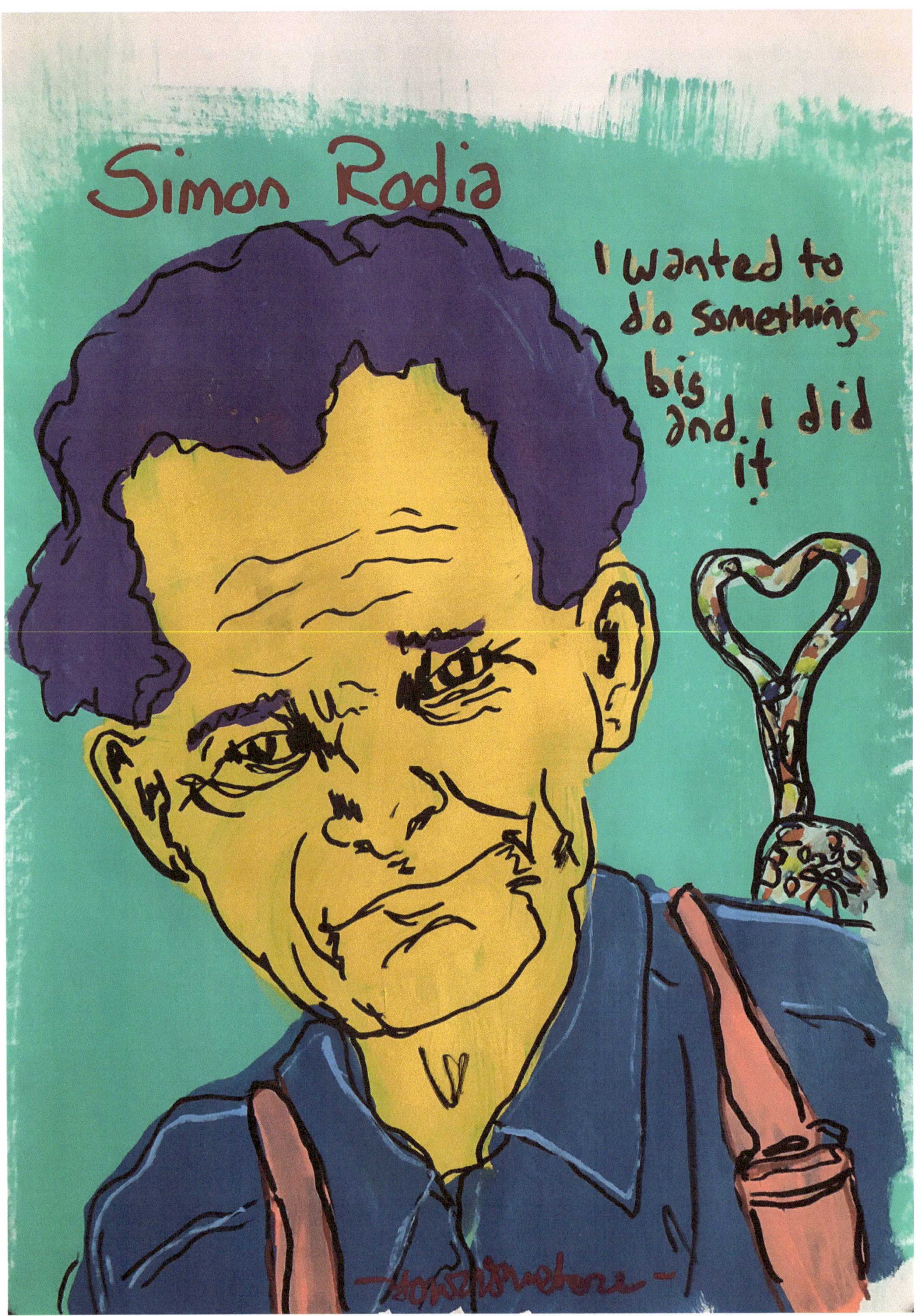

Simon Rodia
I wanted to do something big and I did it

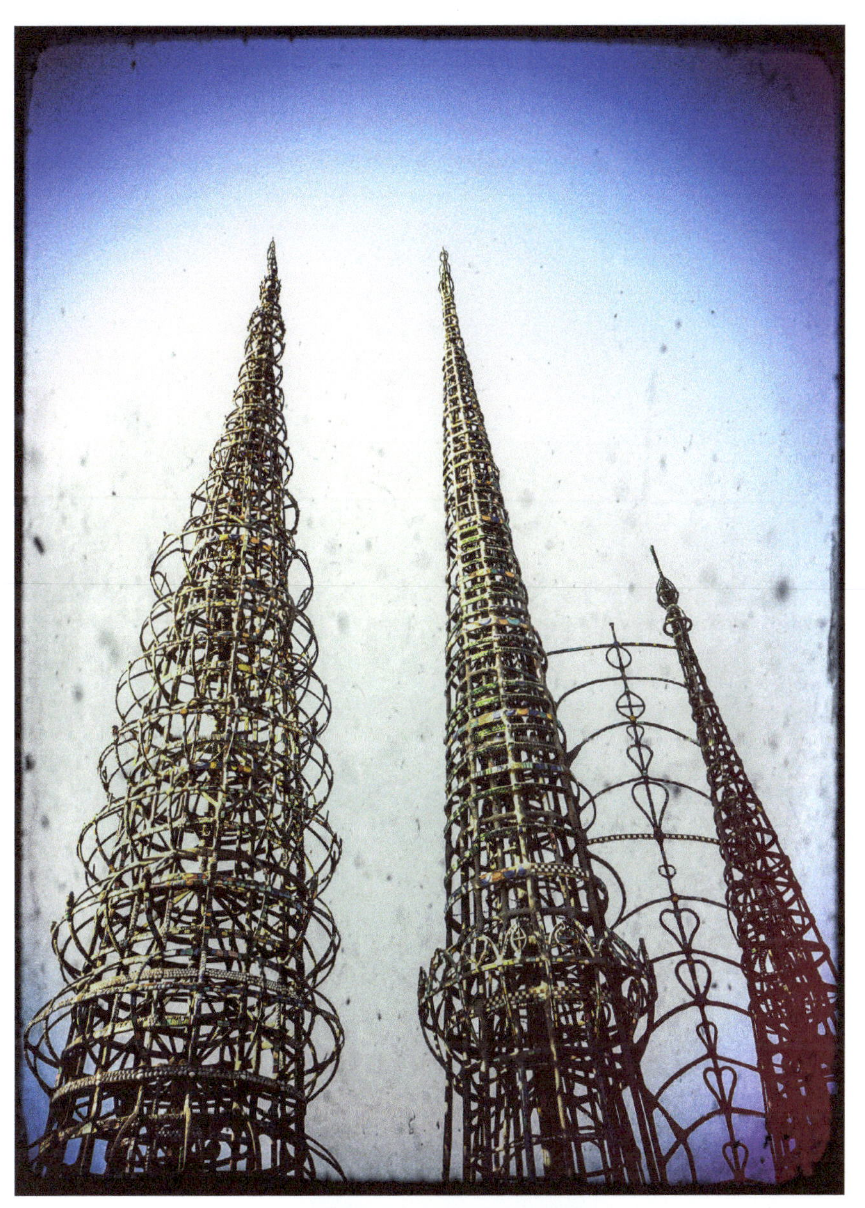

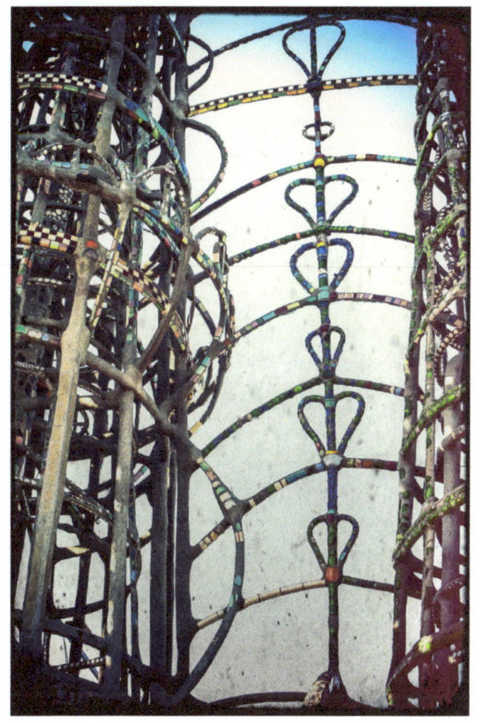

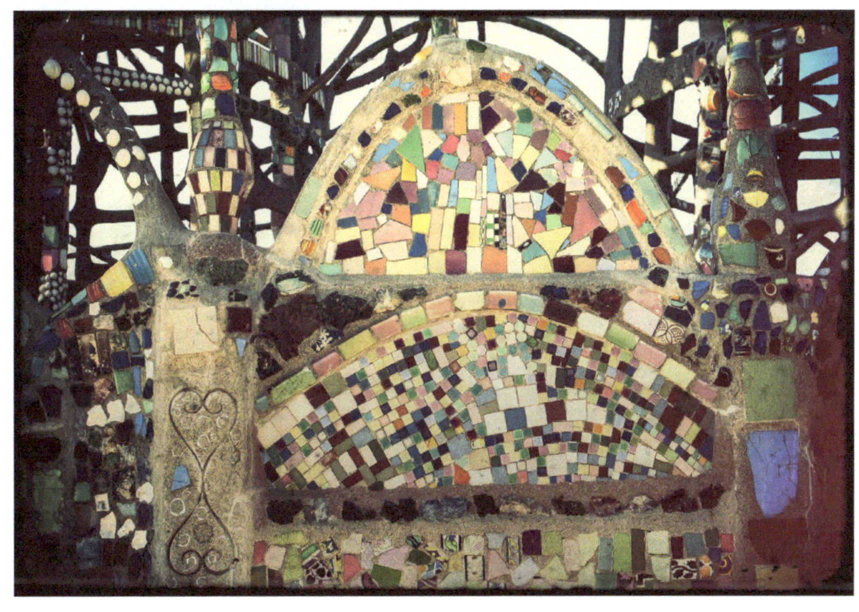

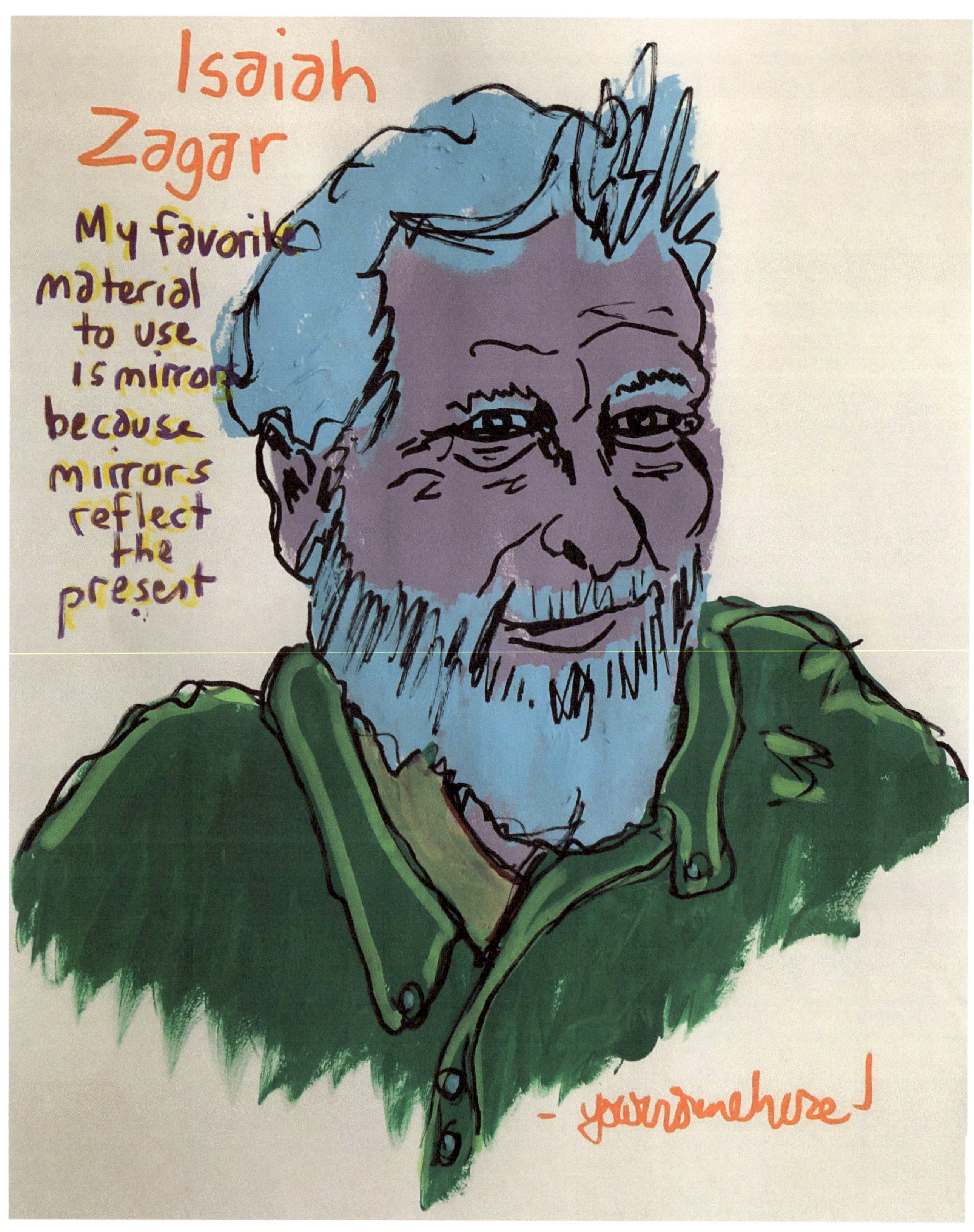

Isaiah
Zagar
My favorite
material
to use
is mirror
because
mirrors
reflect
the
present
- yoursomehere

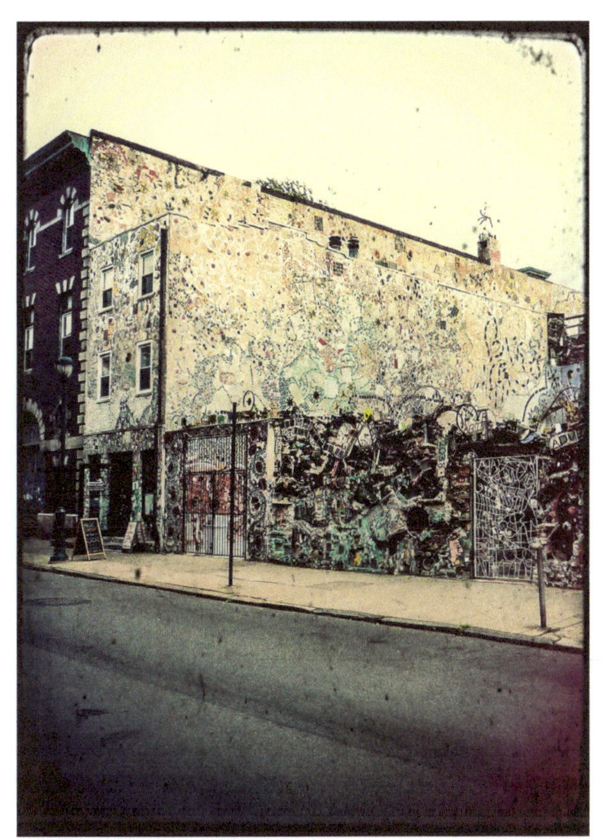

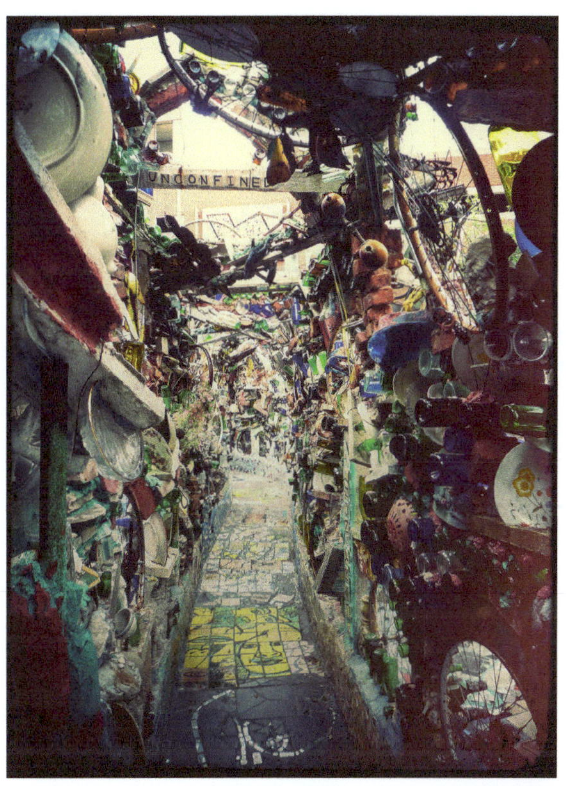
UNCONFINED

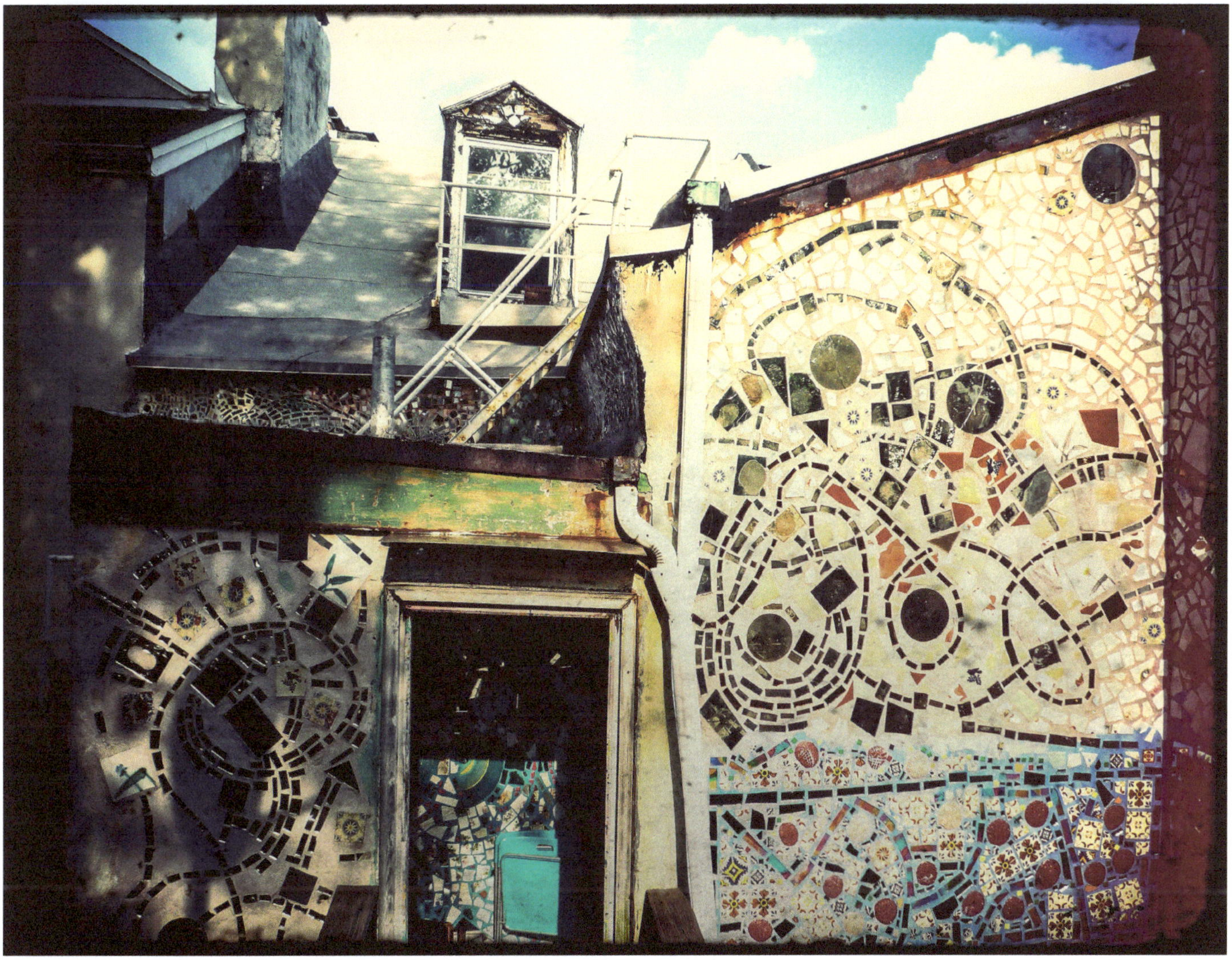

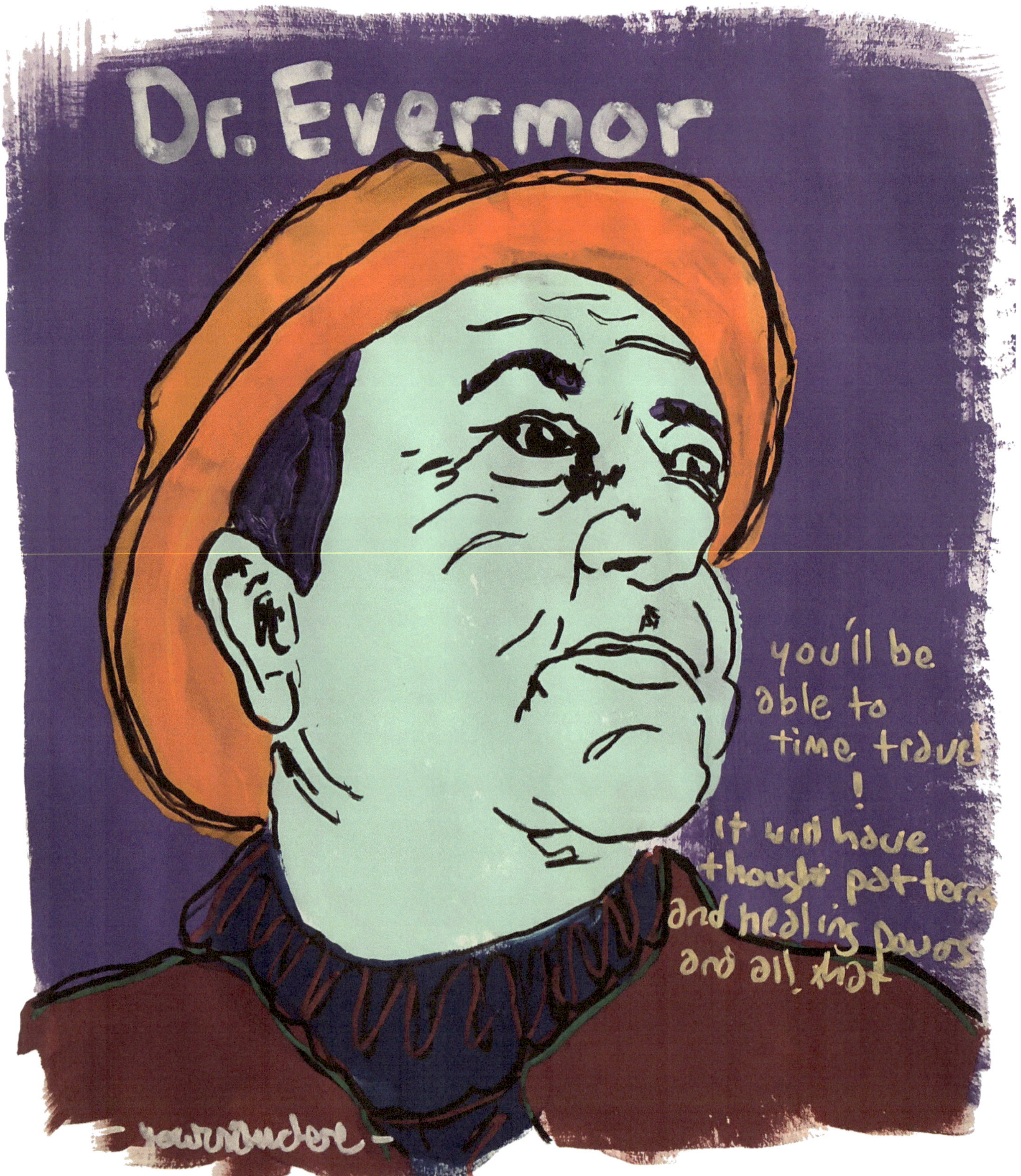

Dr. Evermor
you'll be able to time travel!
it will have thought patterns and healing powers and all that

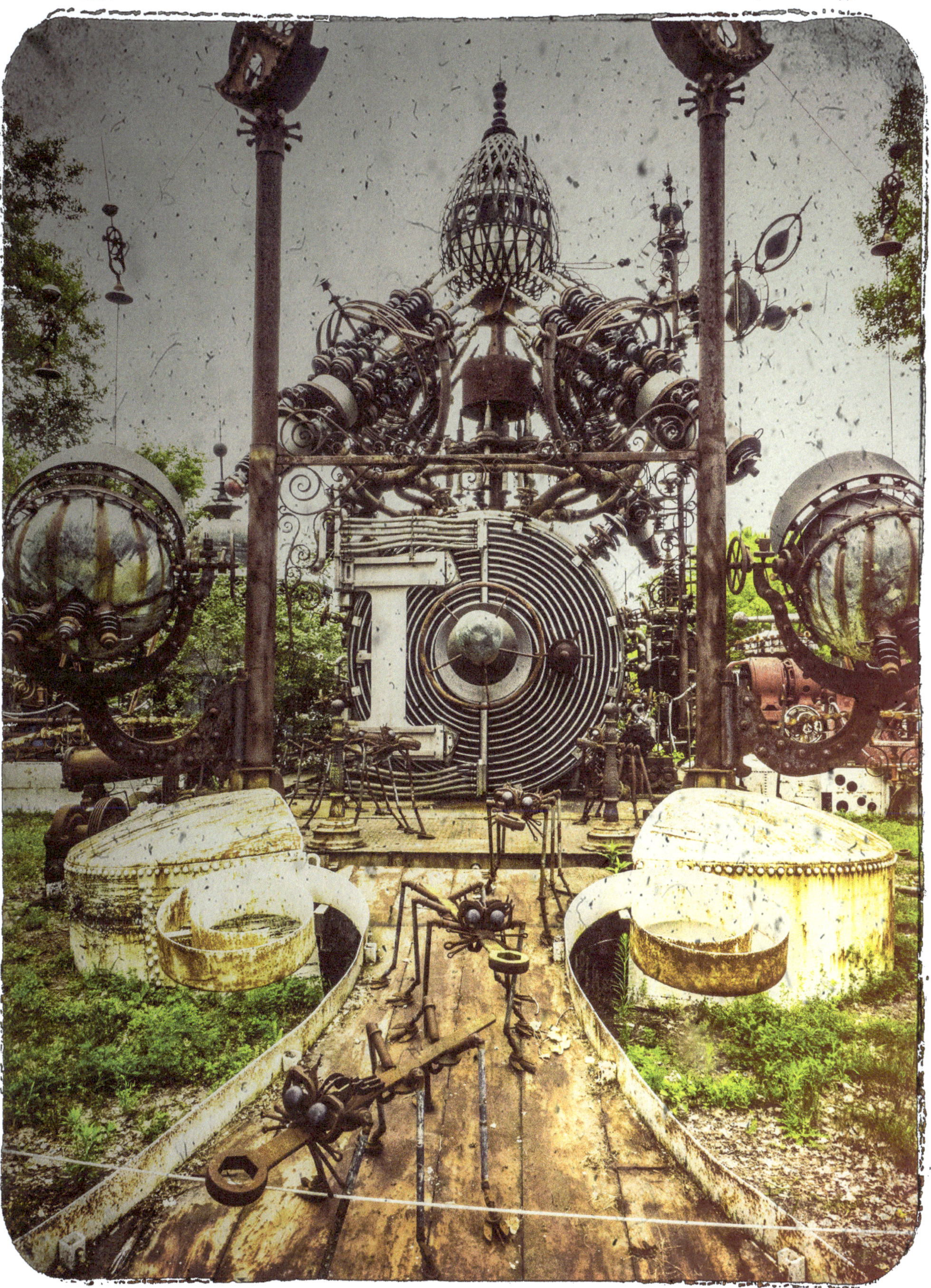

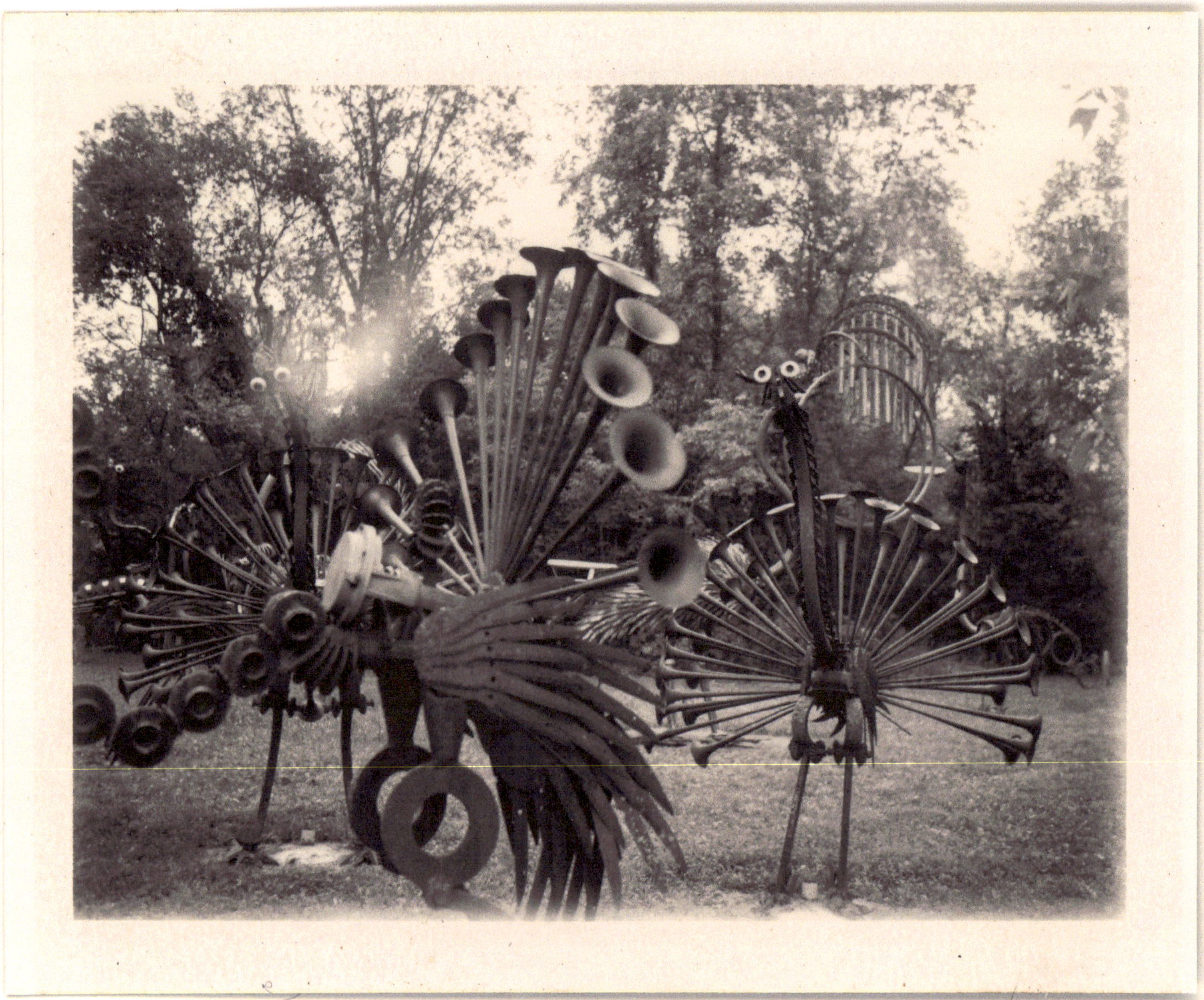

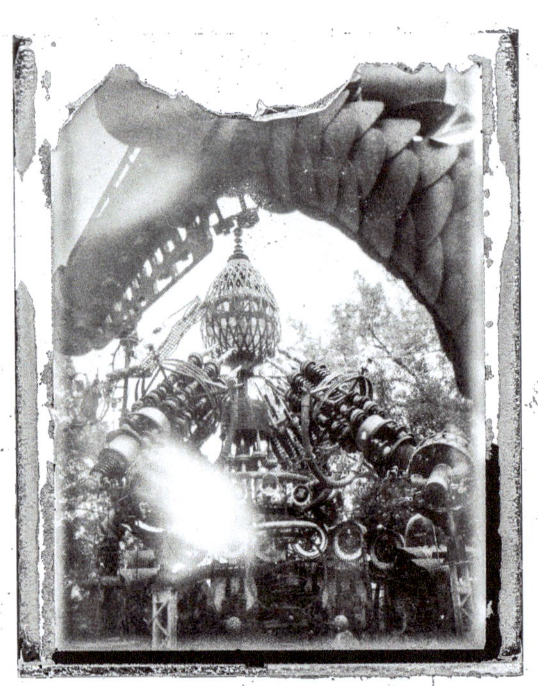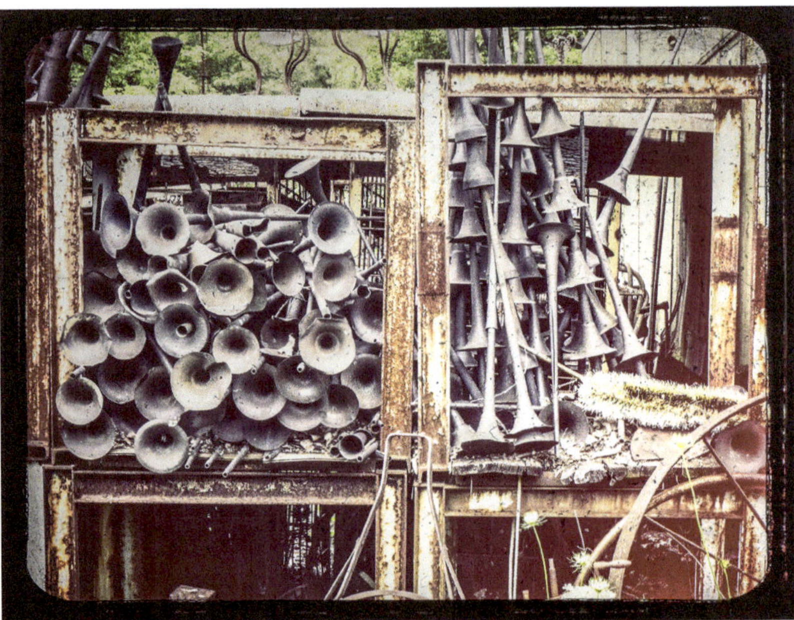

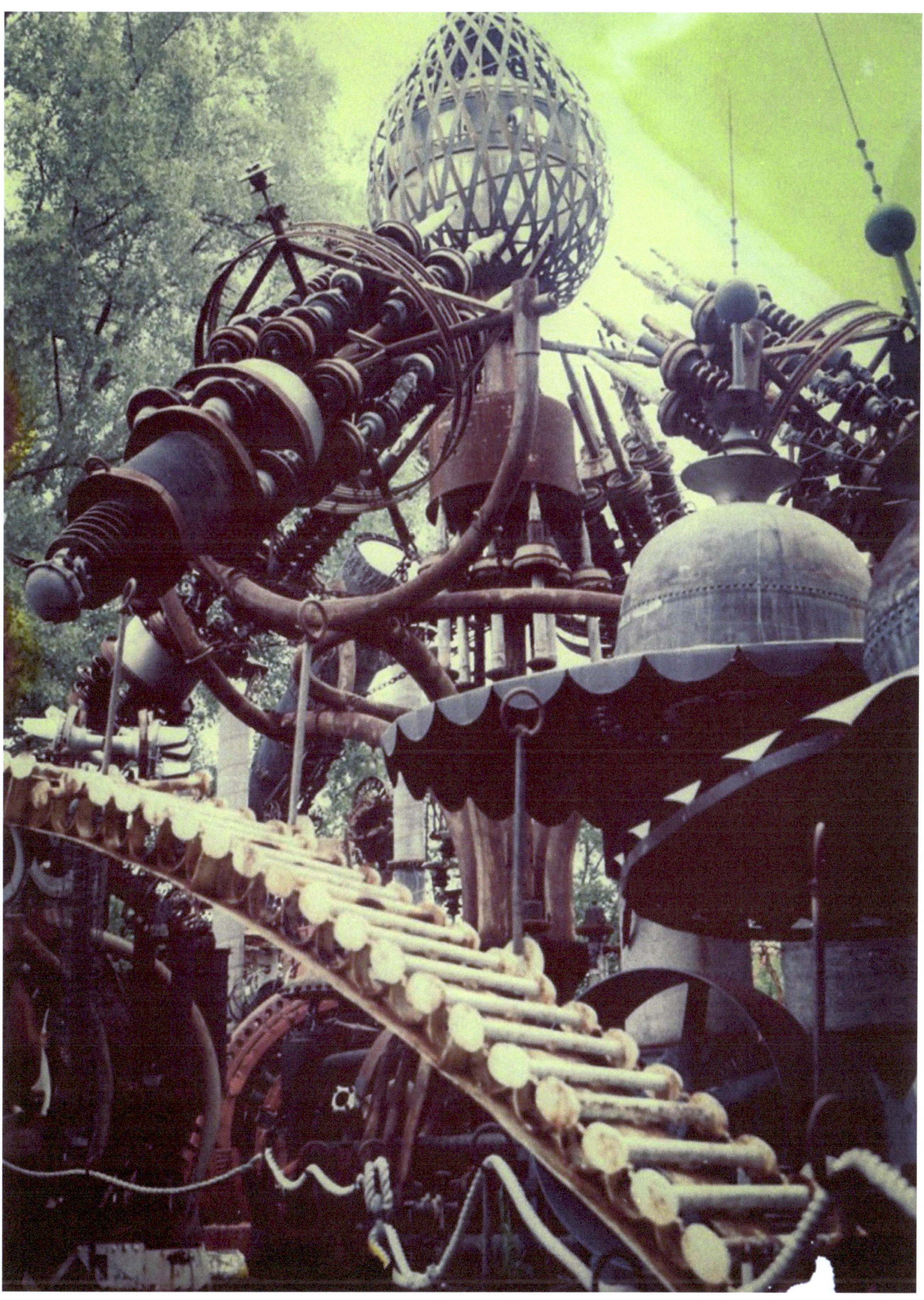

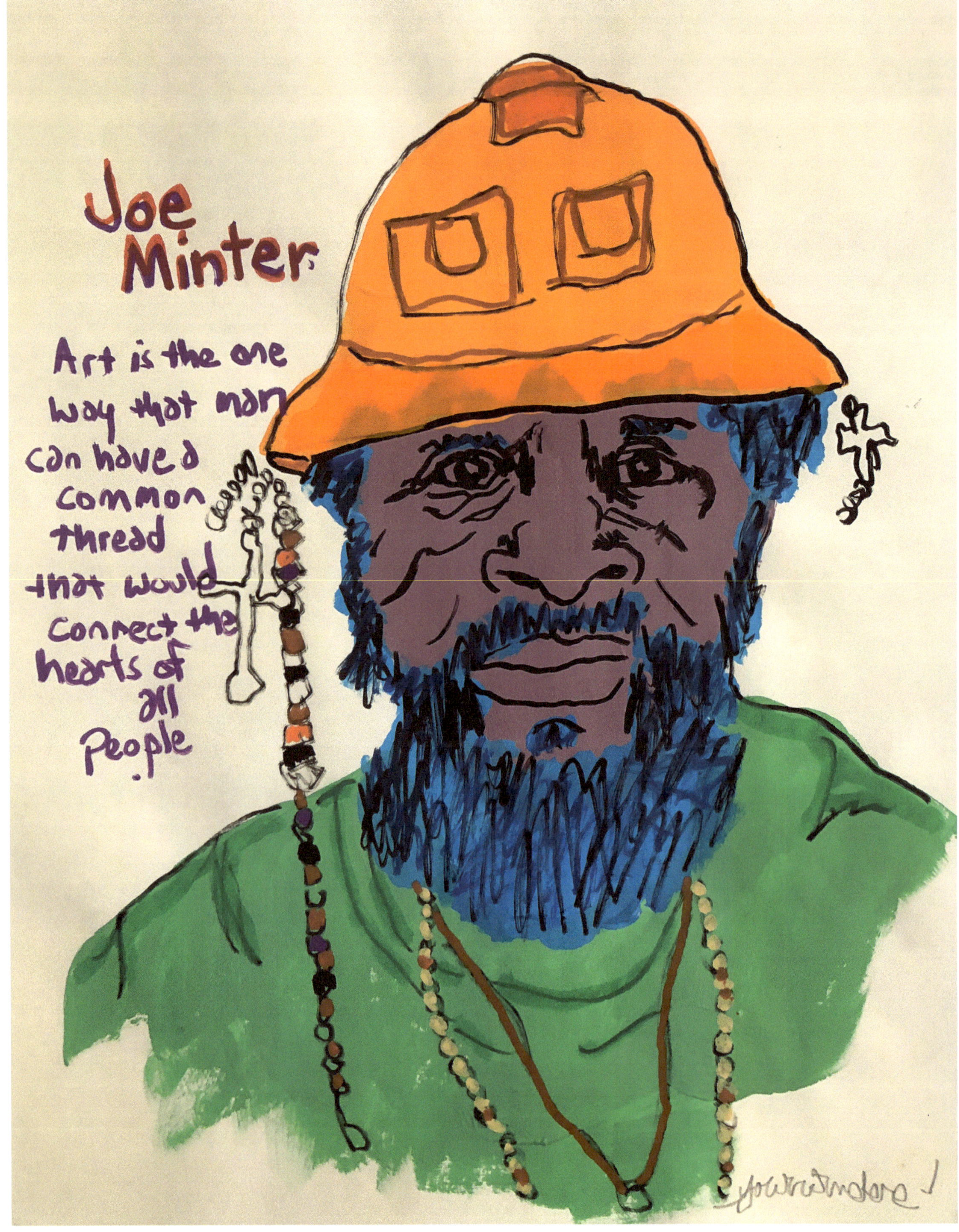
Joe
Minter

Art is the one
way that man
can have a
common
thread
that would
connect the
hearts of
all
People
.

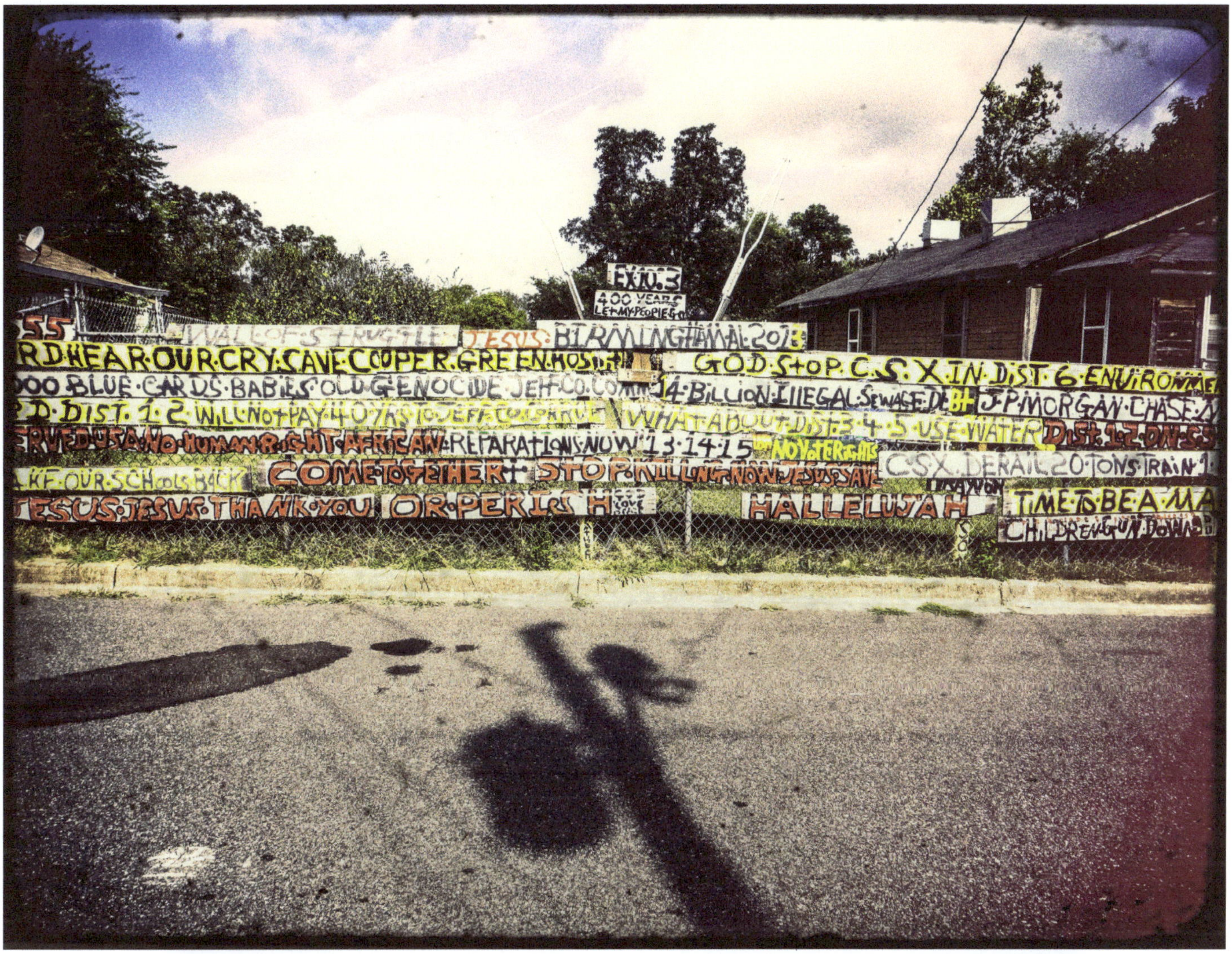

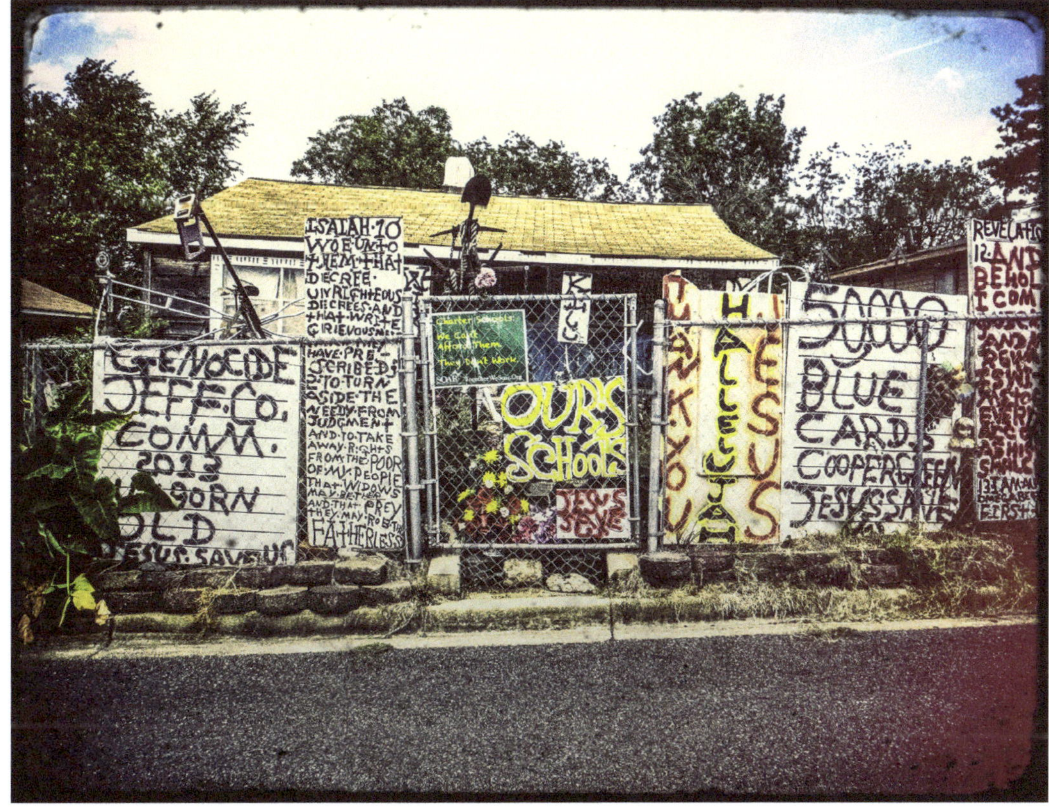

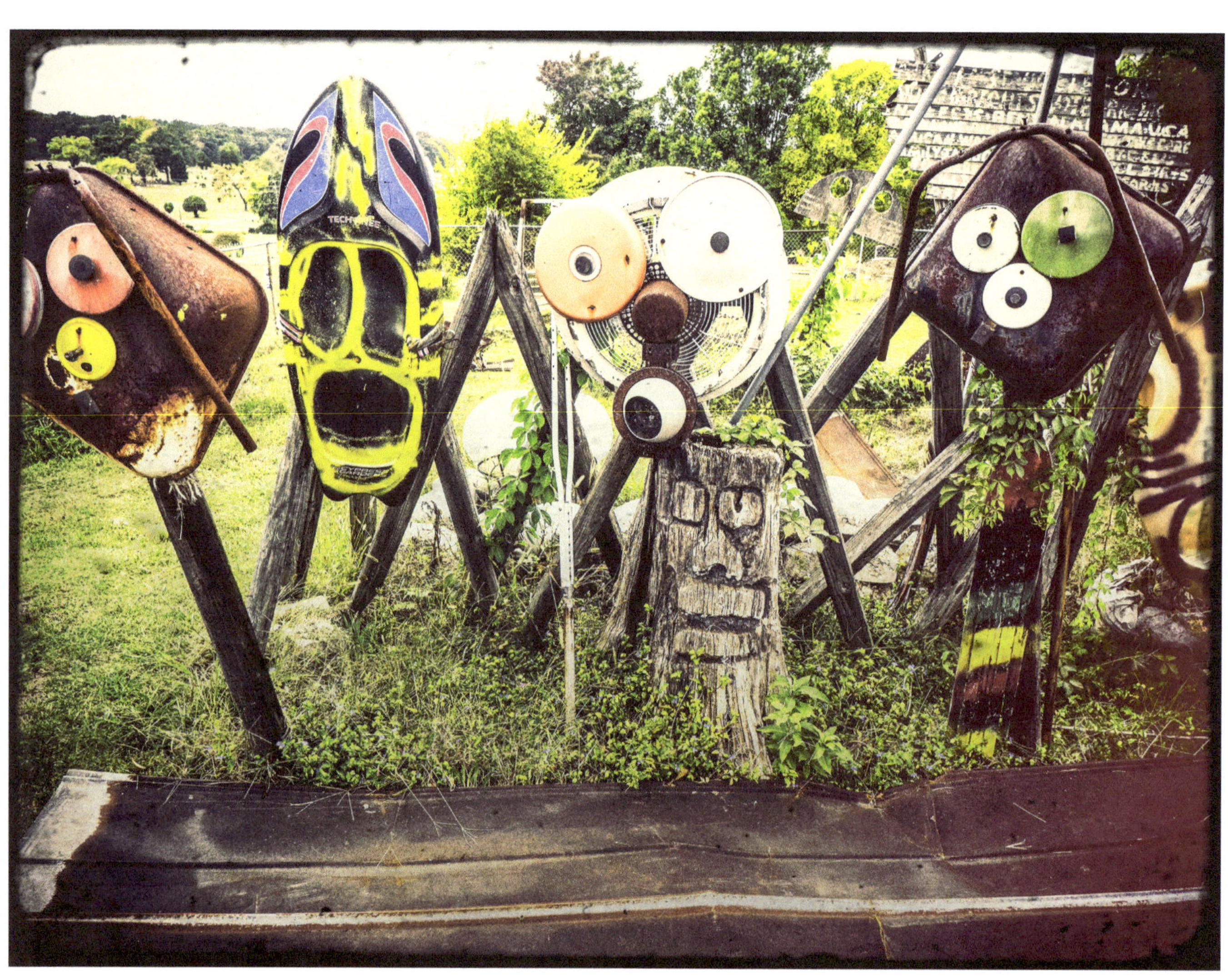

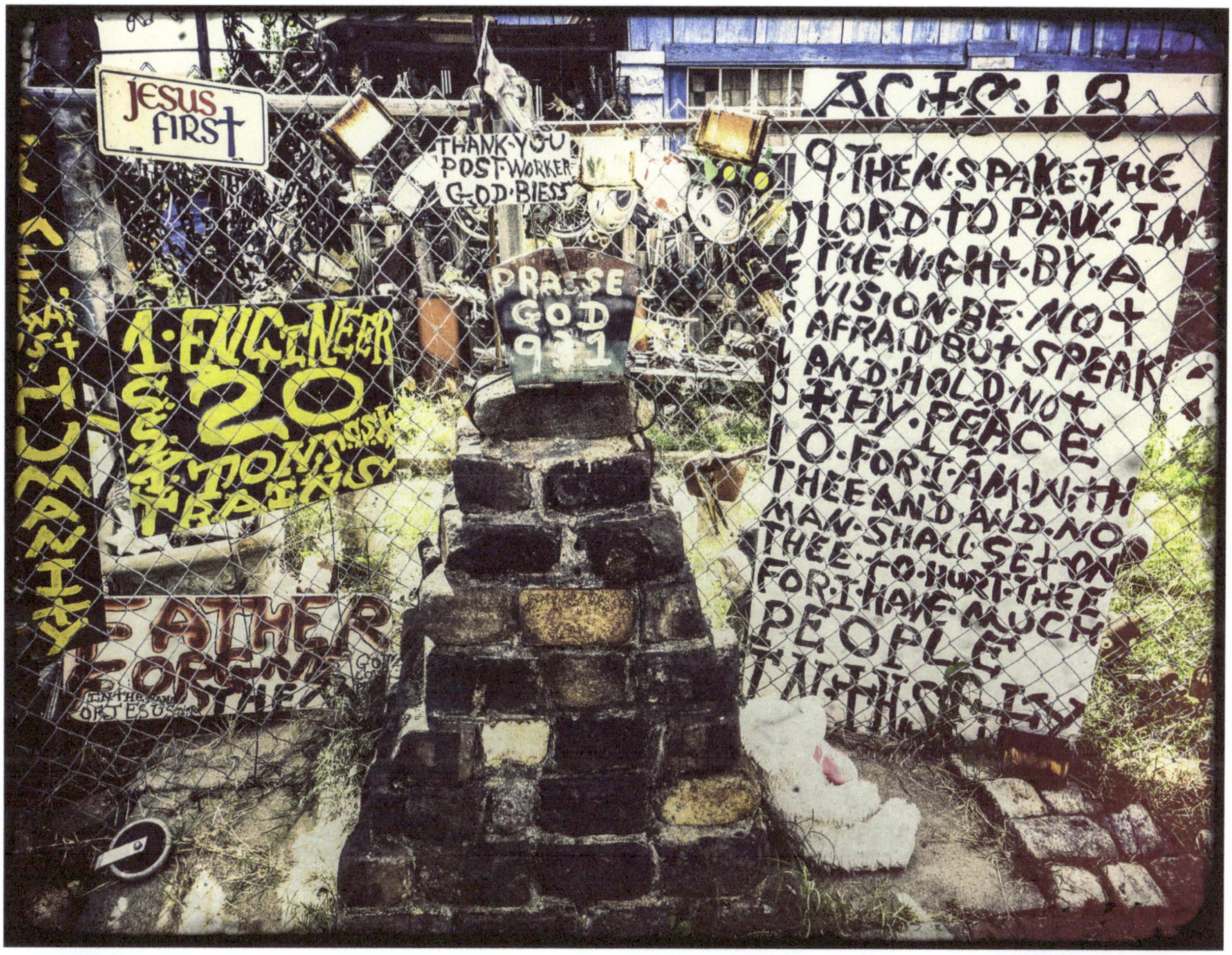

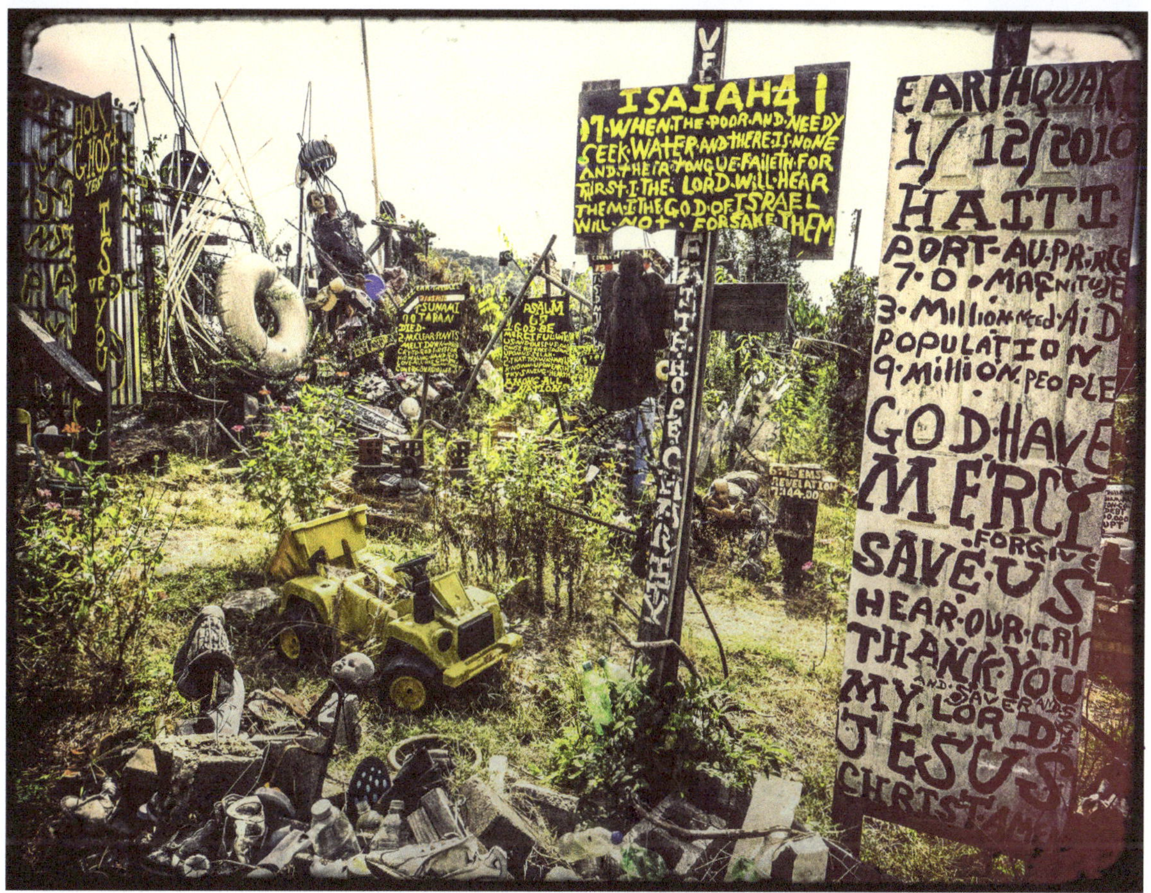
Jesus FIRST
THANK YOU POST WORKER GOD BLESS
PRAISE GOD 911
1 ENGINEER 20 TRAINS
FATHER
ACTS 18
9 THEN SPAKE THE LORD TO PAUL IN THE NIGHT BY A VISION BE NOT AFRAID BUT SPEAK AND HOLD NOT THY PEACE
10 FOR I AM WITH THEE AND NO MAN SHALL SET ON THEE TO HURT THEE FOR I HAVE MUCH PEOPLE IN THIS CITY
ISAIAH 41
17 WHEN THE POOR AND NEEDY SEEK WATER AND THERE IS NONE AND THEIR TONGUE FAILETH FOR THIRST I THE LORD WILL HEAR THEM I THE GOD OF ISRAEL WILL NOT FORSAKE THEM
EARTHQUAKE 1/12/2010 HAITI PORT-AU-PRINCE 7.0 MAGNITUDE 3 MILLION NEED AID POPULATION 9 MILLION PEOPLE
GOD HAVE MERCY FORGIVE SAVE US HEAR OUR CRY THANK YOU MY LORD JESUS CHRIST
HOLY GHOST YES
I LOVE YOU

Samuel P. Dinsmoor

He called his Garden of Eden the most unique home for living or dead on earth

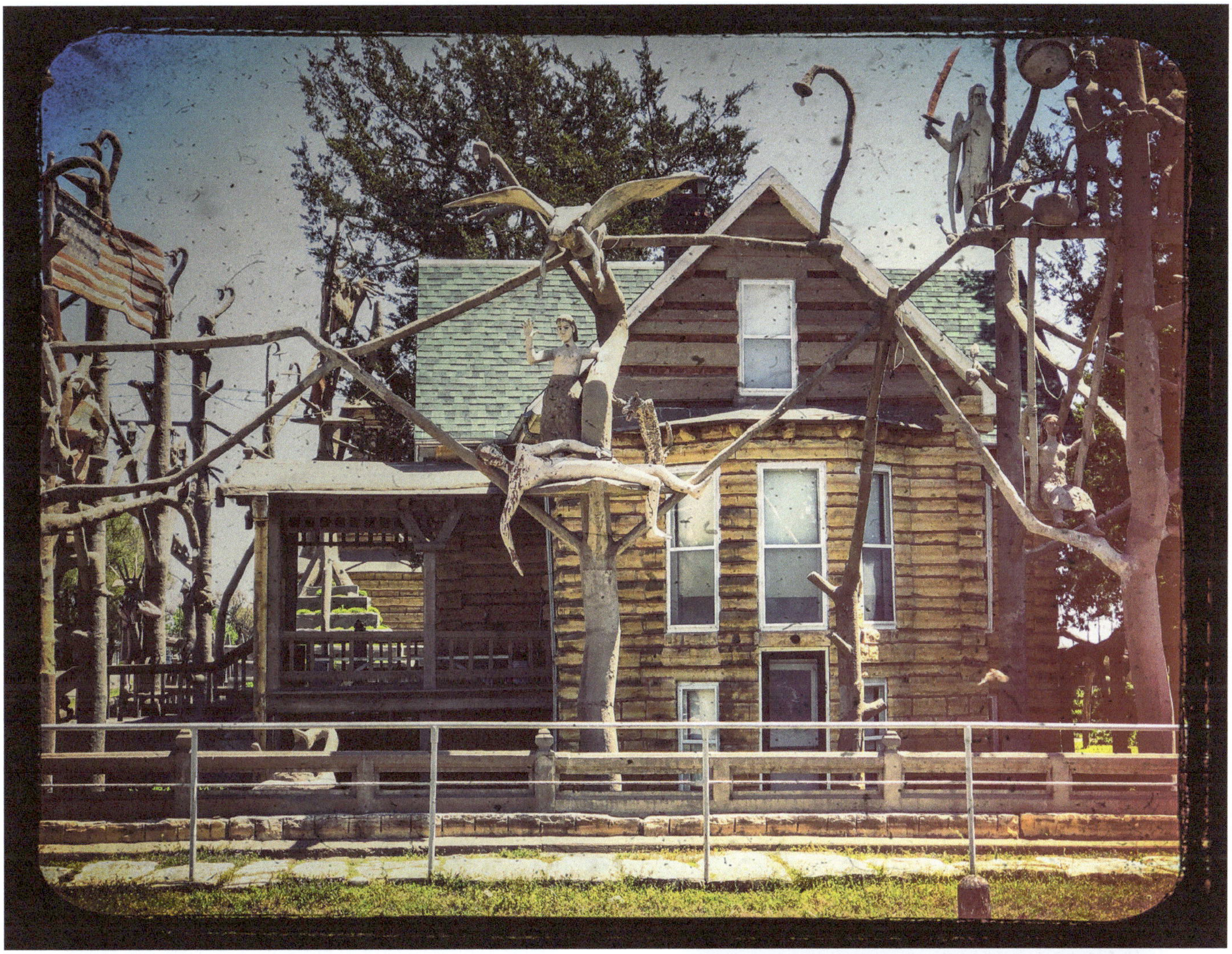

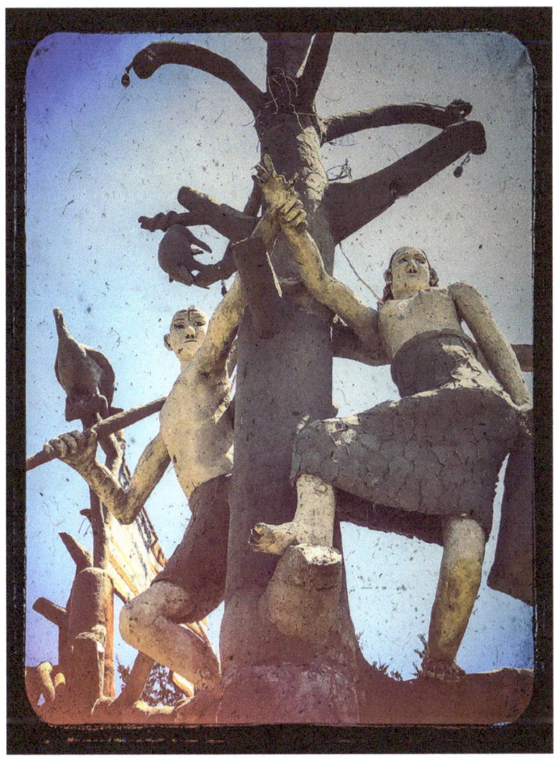

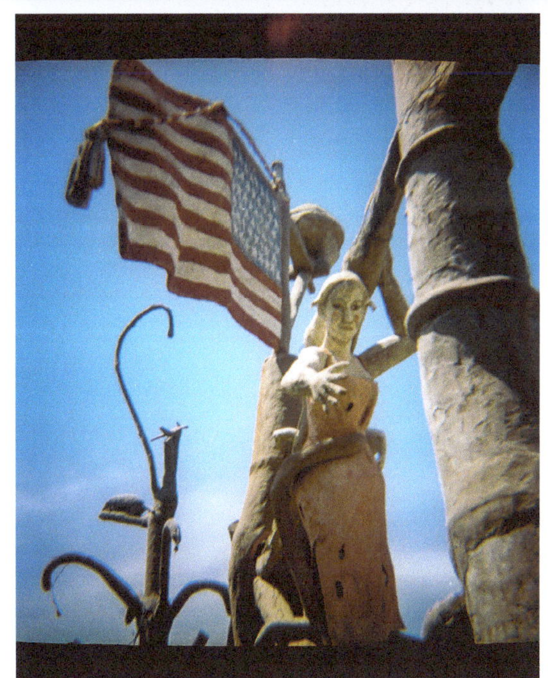

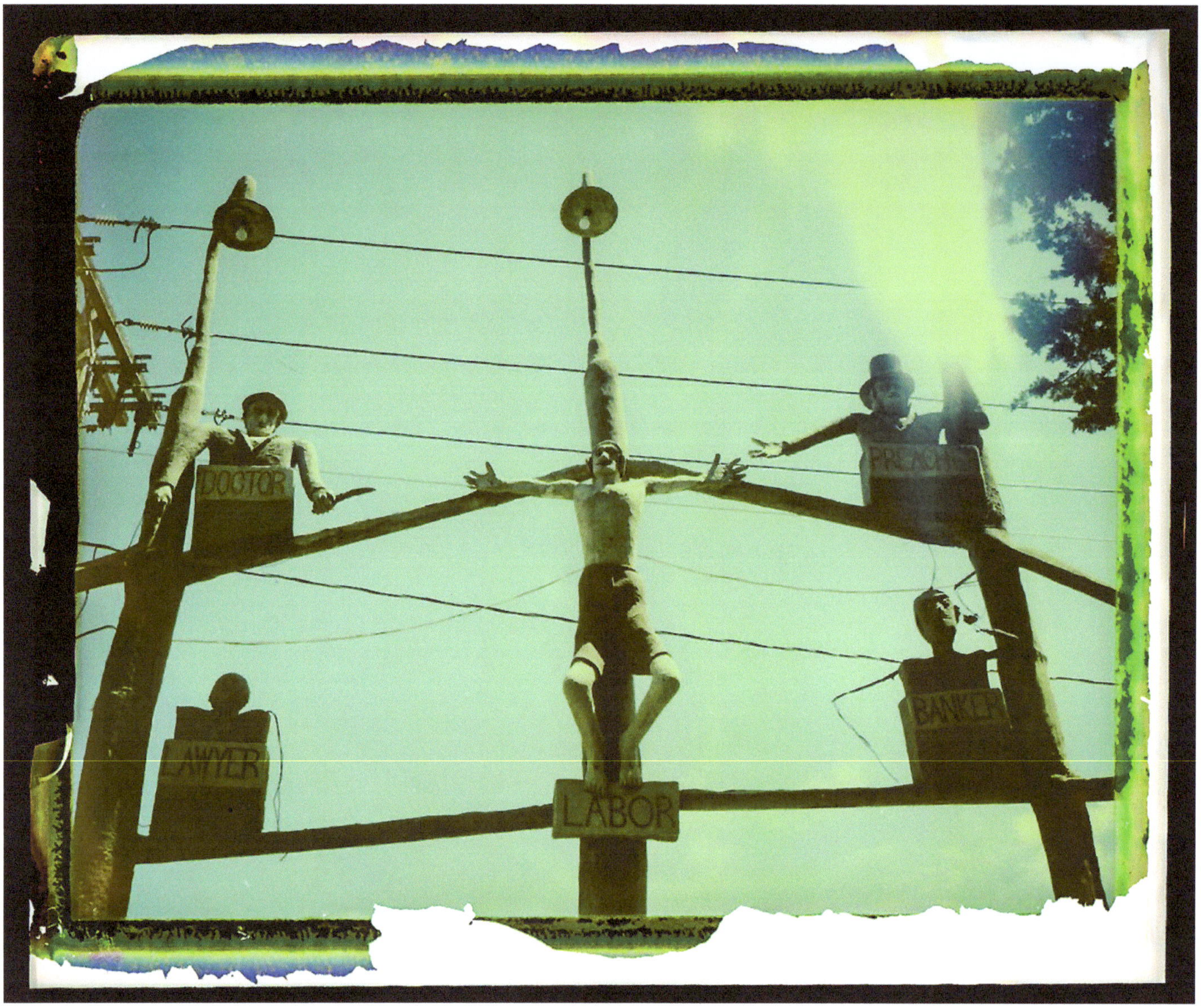

DOCTOR
PREACHER
LAWYER
BANKER
LABOR

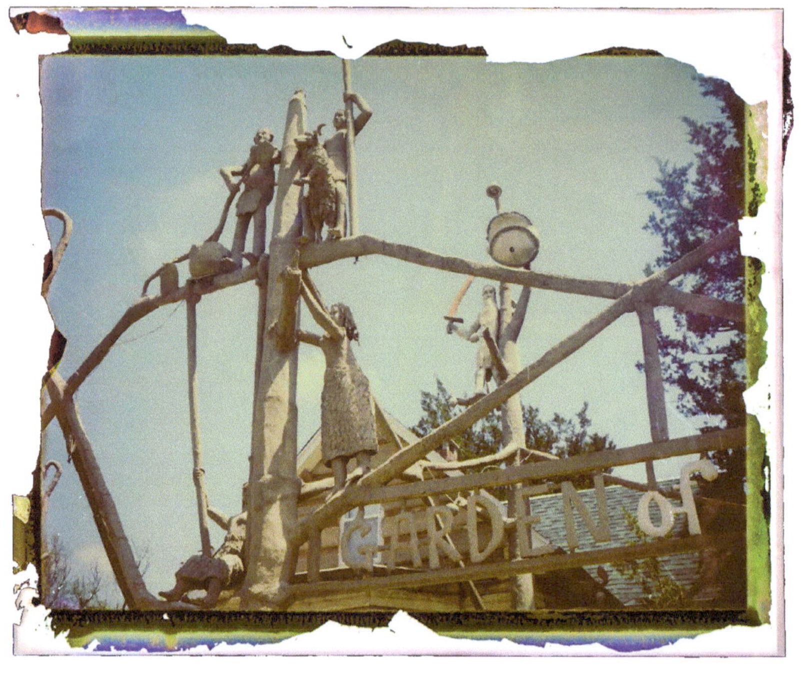

GARDEN of

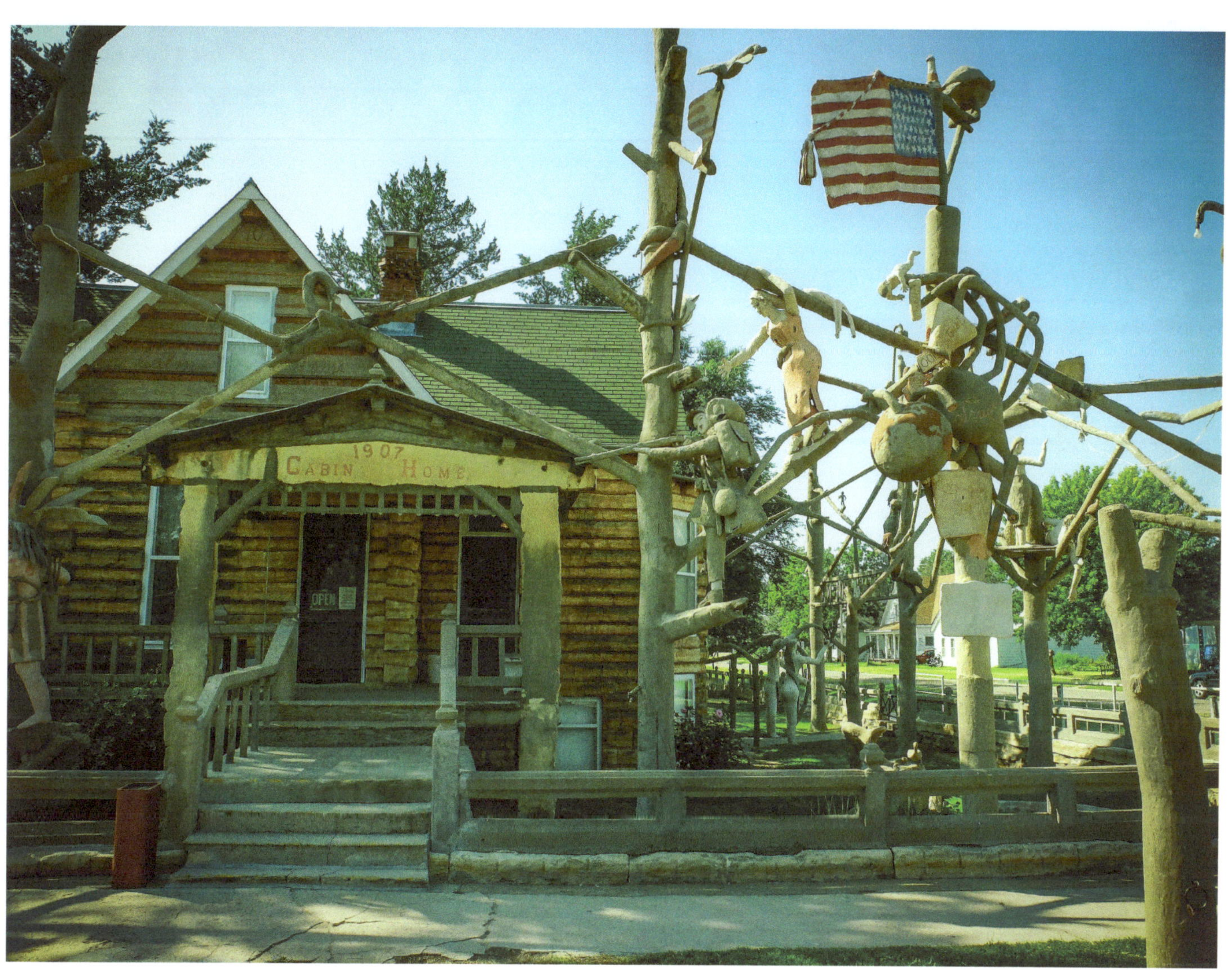

1907
CABIN HOME
OPEN

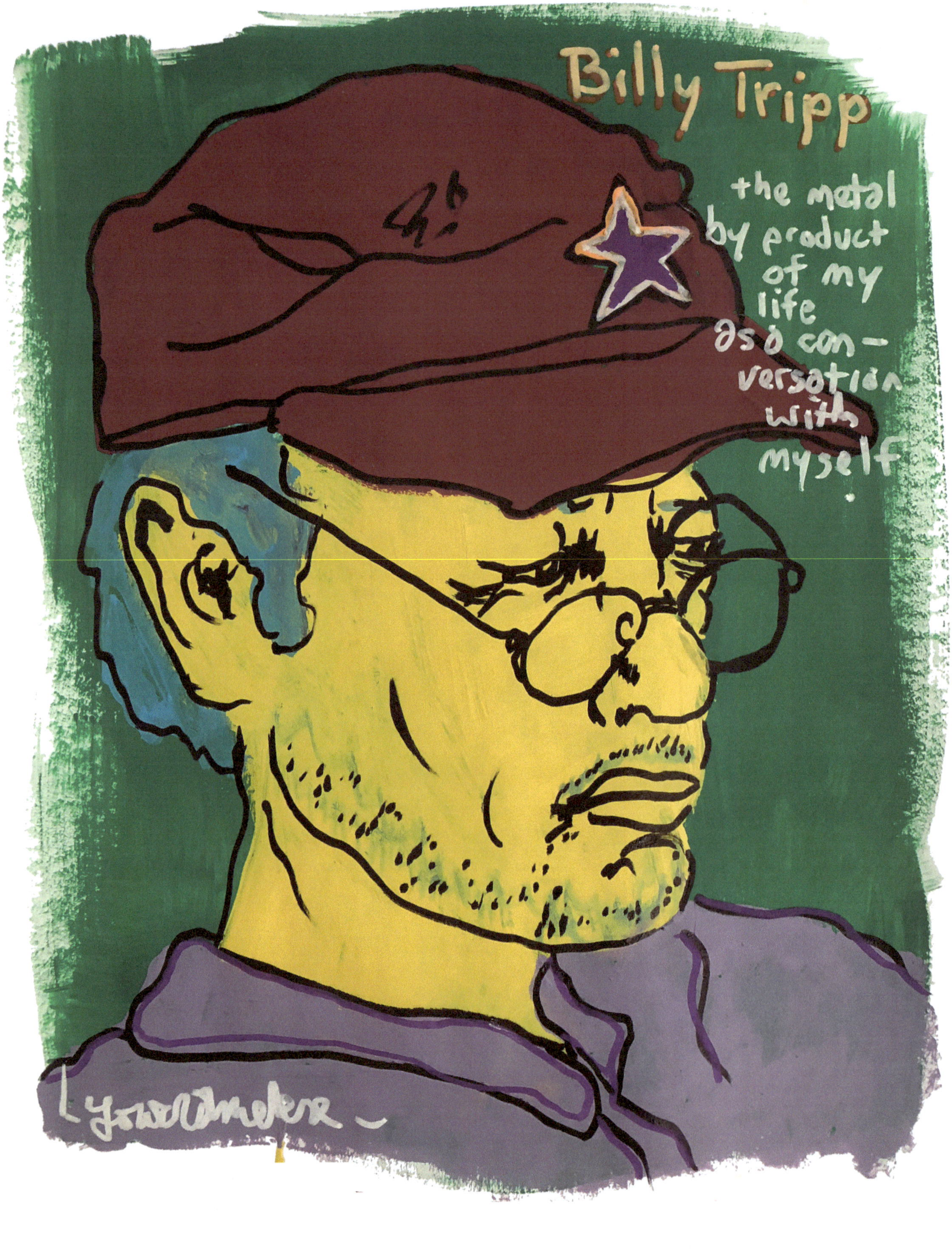

Billy Tripp
the metal
by product
of my
life
as a con-
versation
with
myself

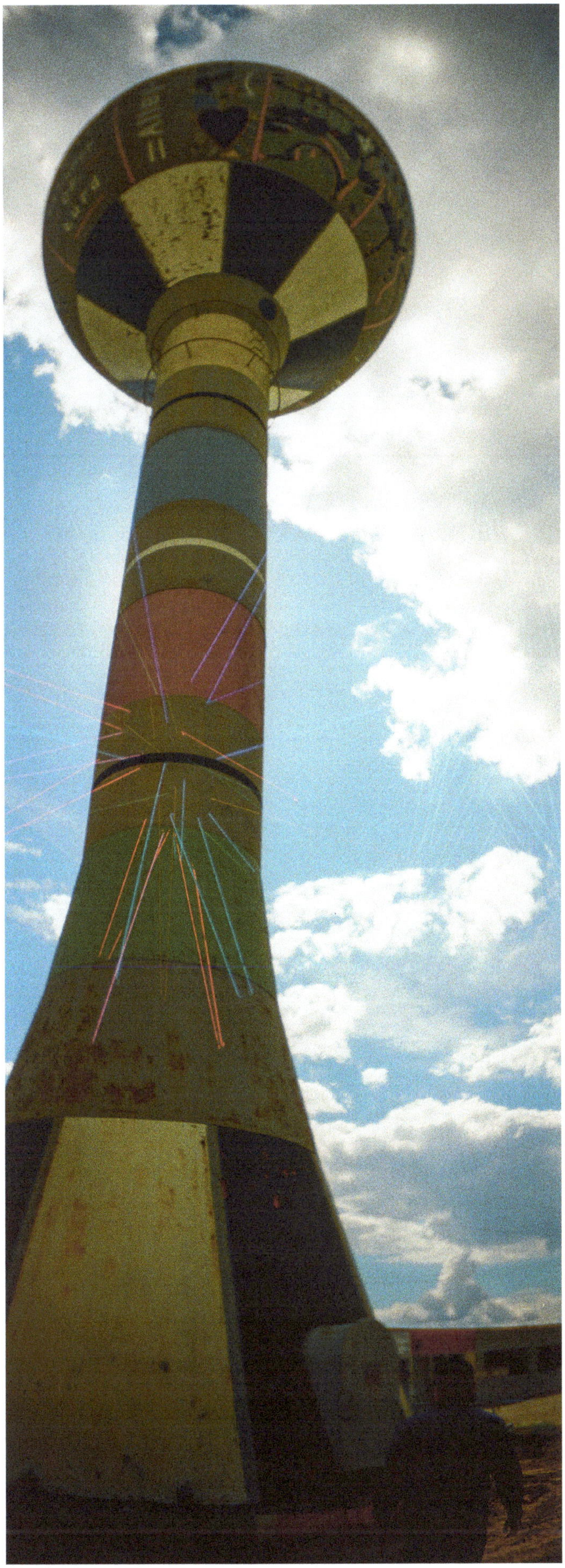

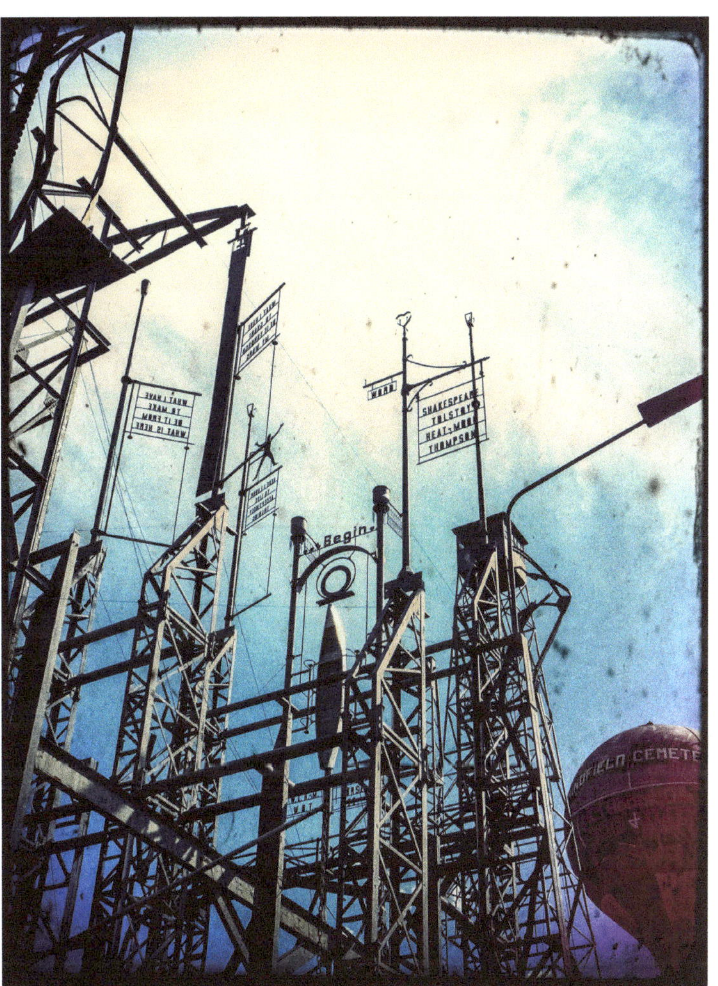
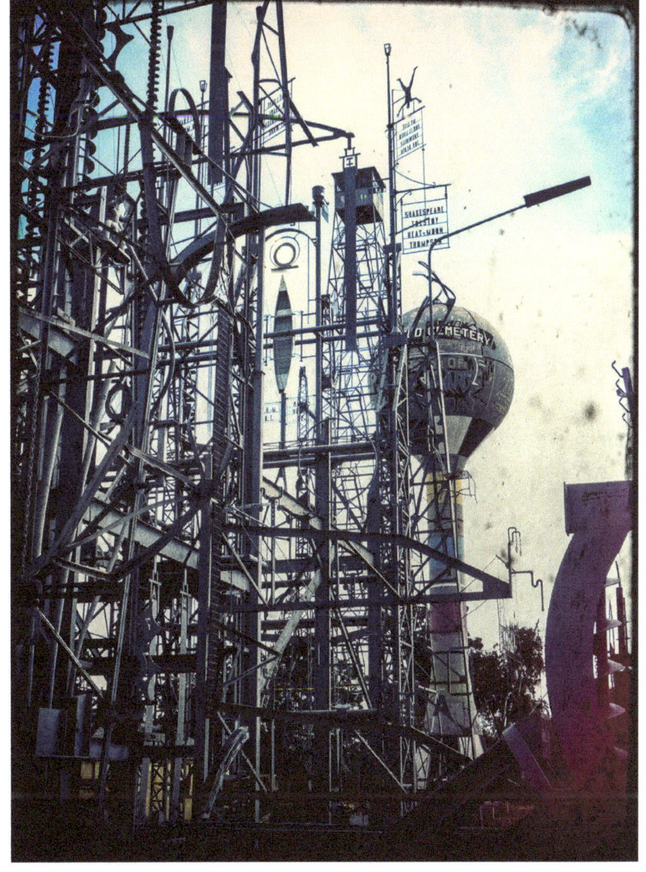

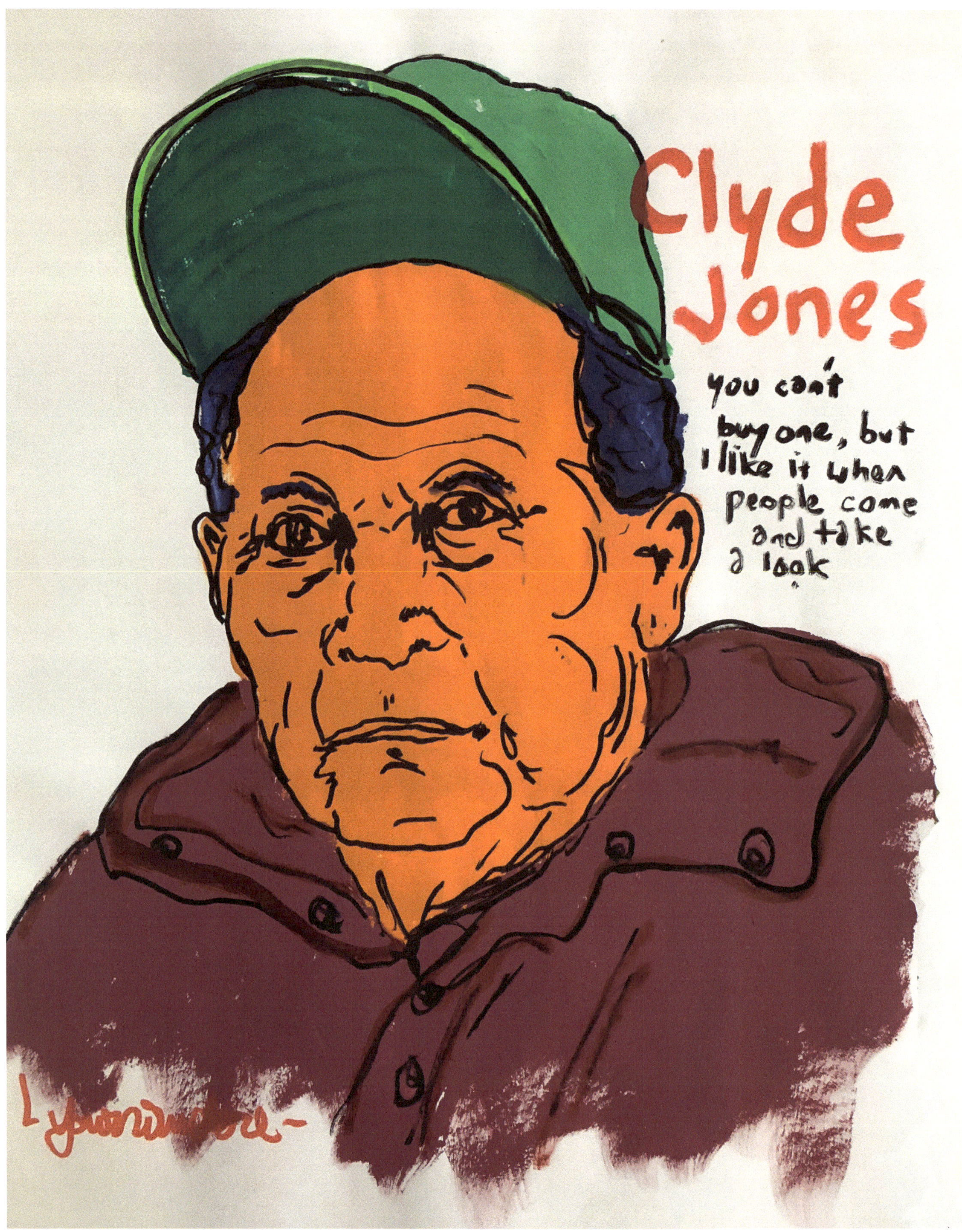
Clyde Jones
you can't buy one, but I like it when people come and take a look

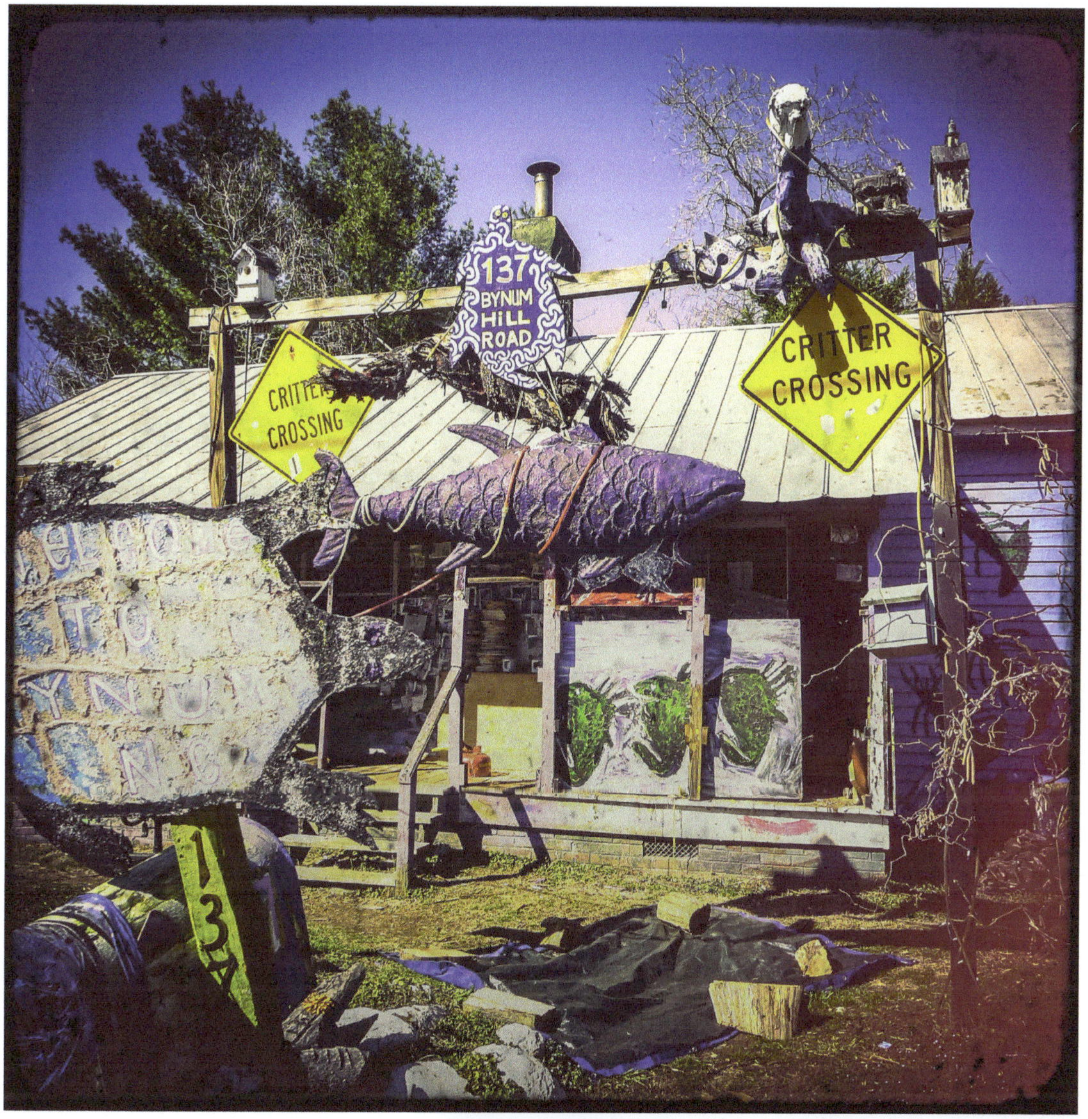

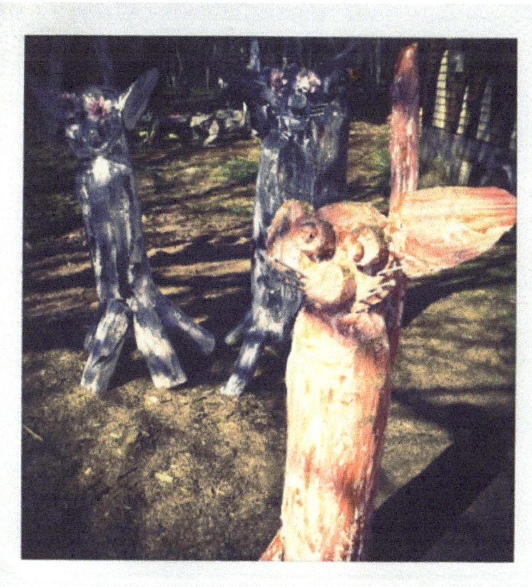

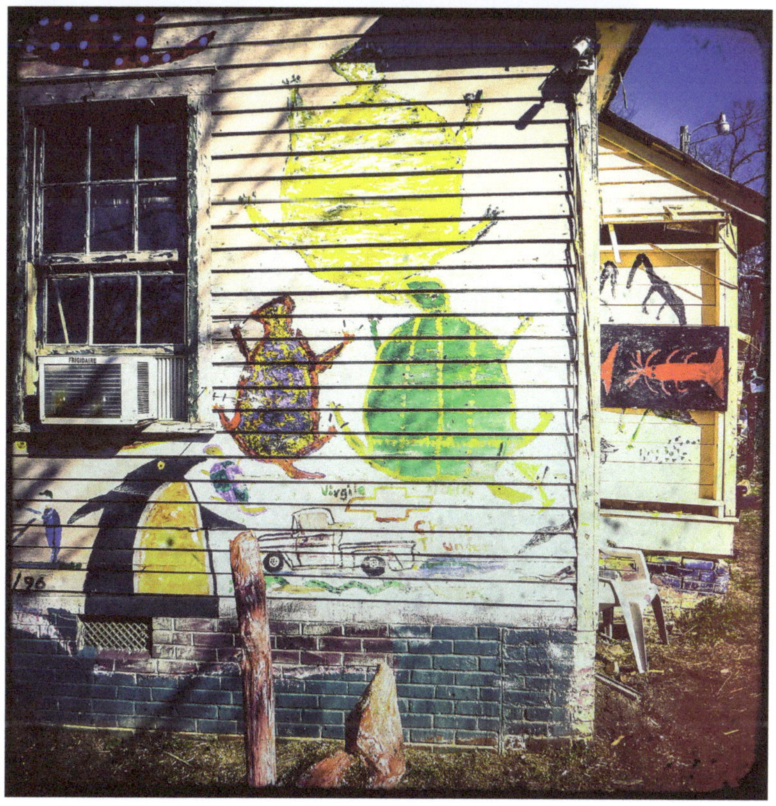
Virgil

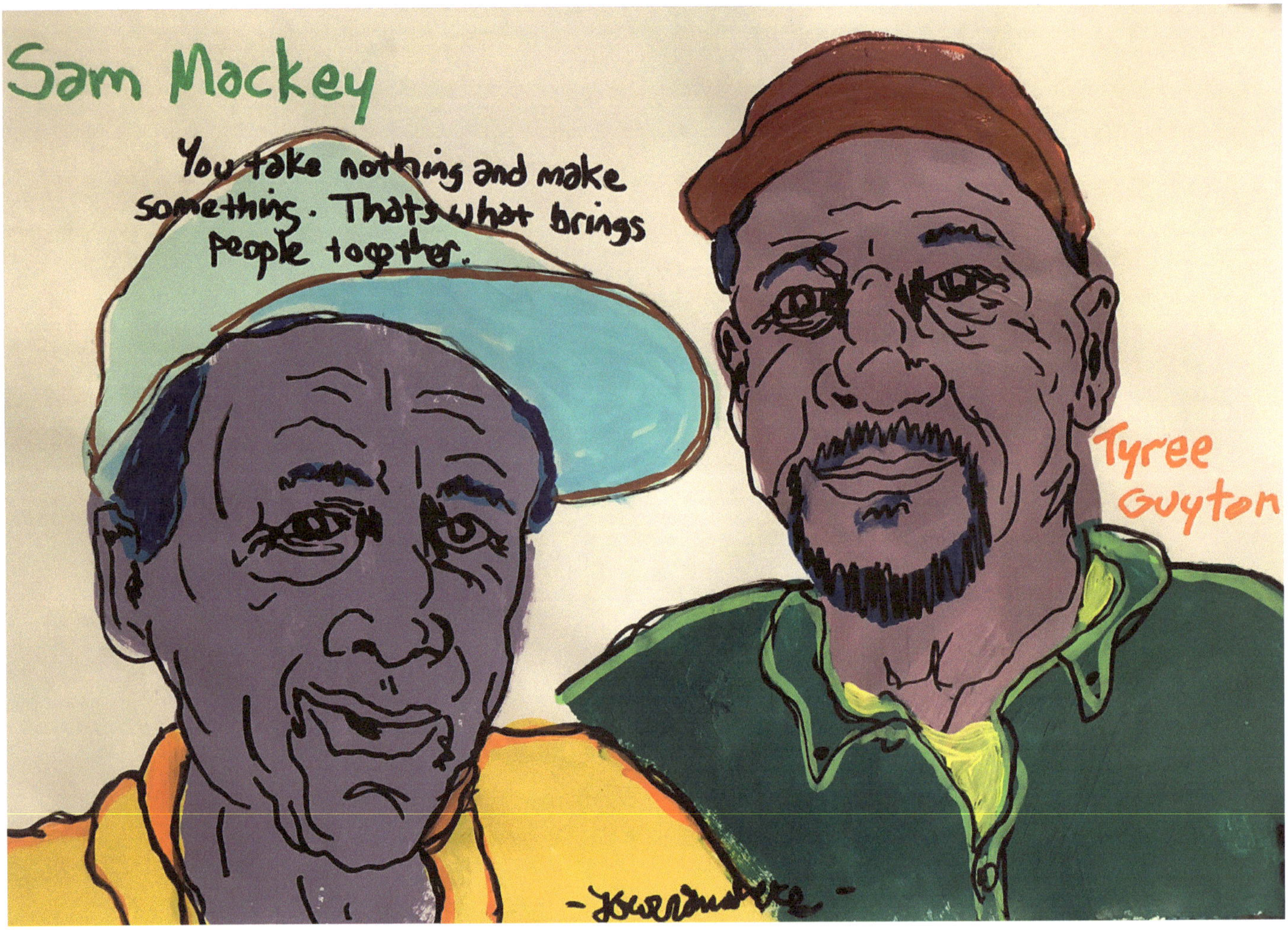

Sam Mackey

You take nothing and make something. Thats what brings people together.

Tyree Guyton

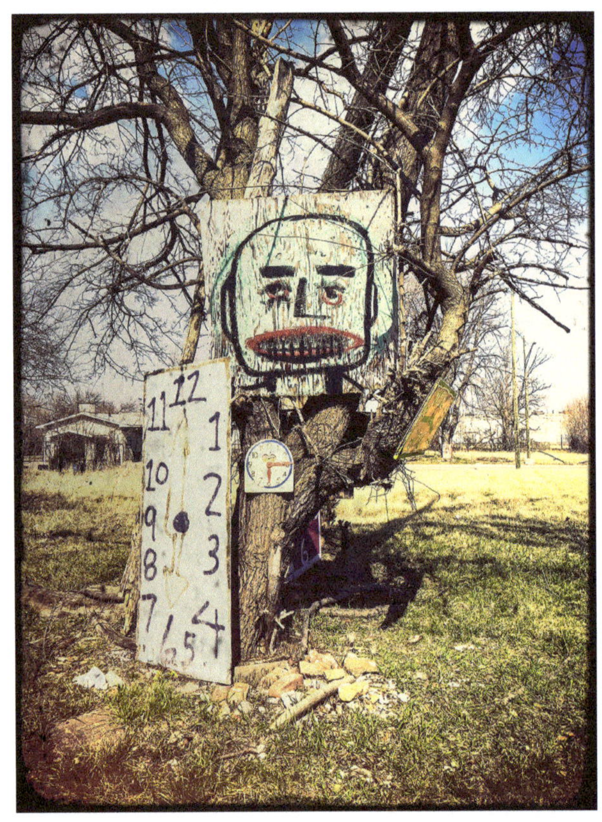

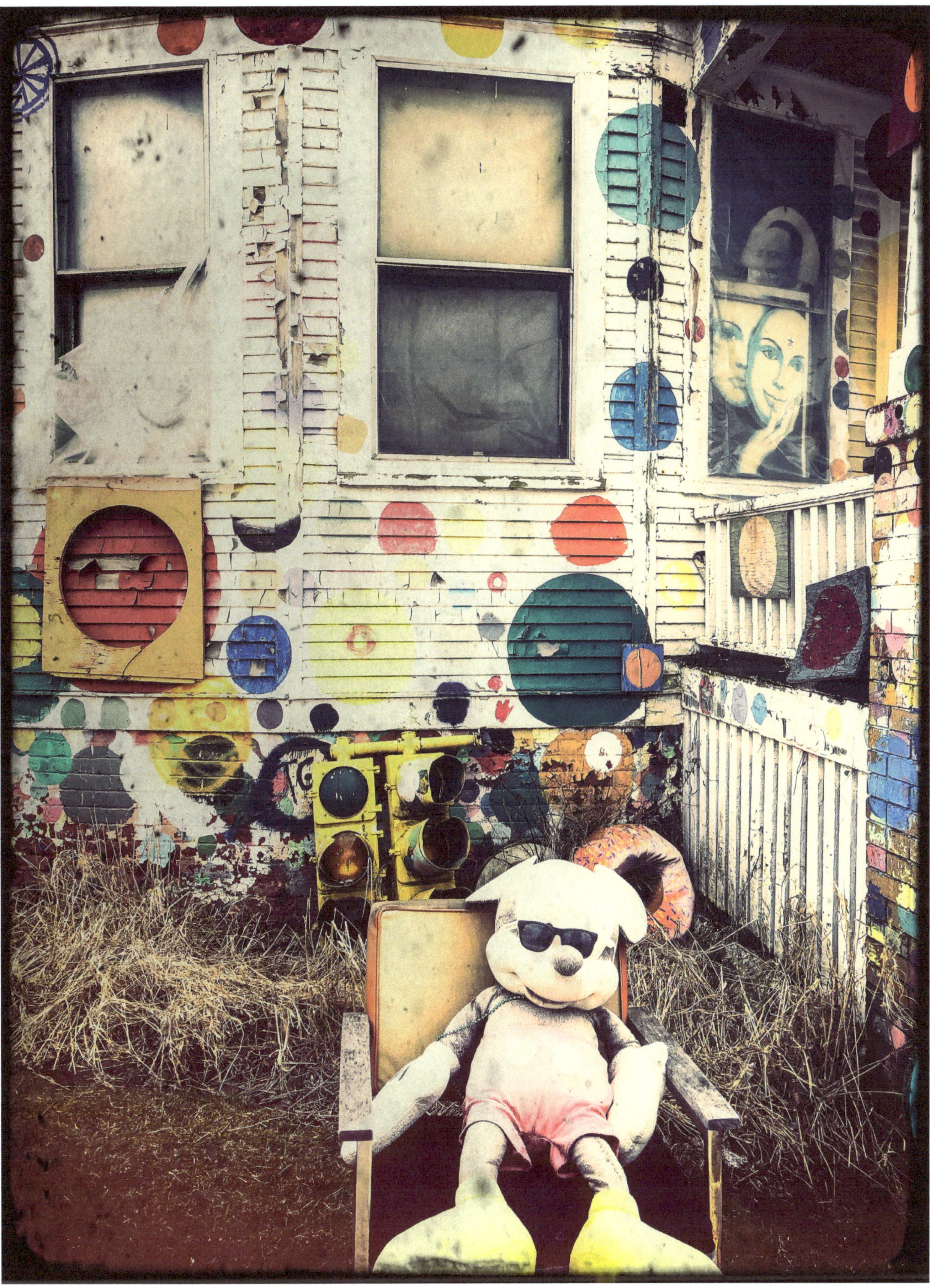

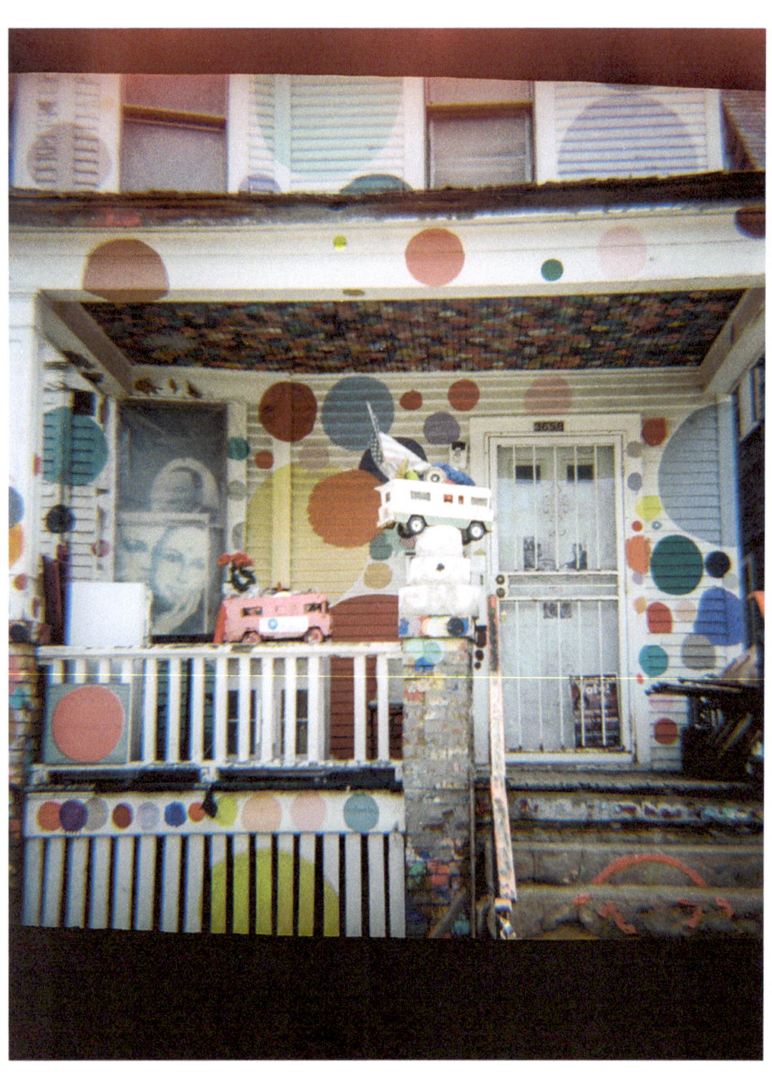

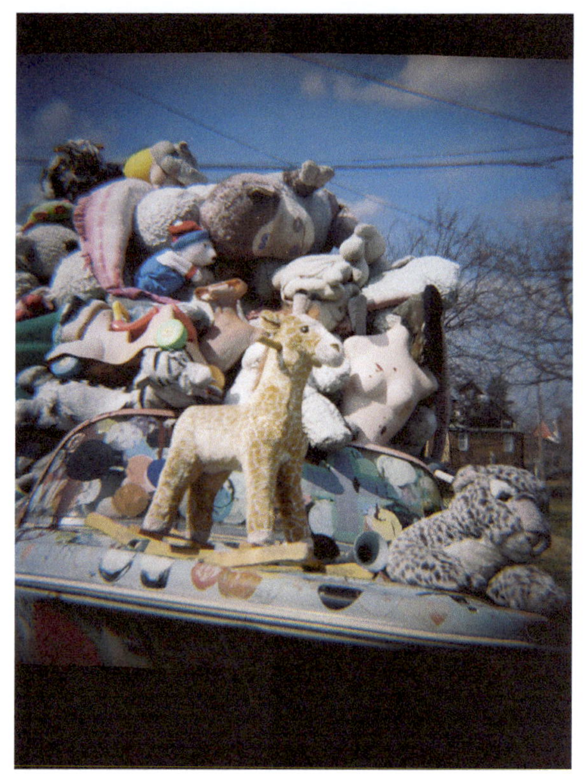

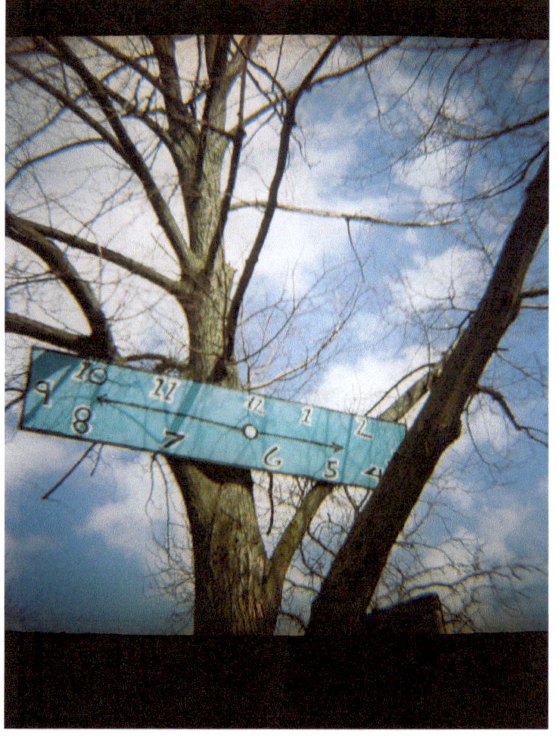

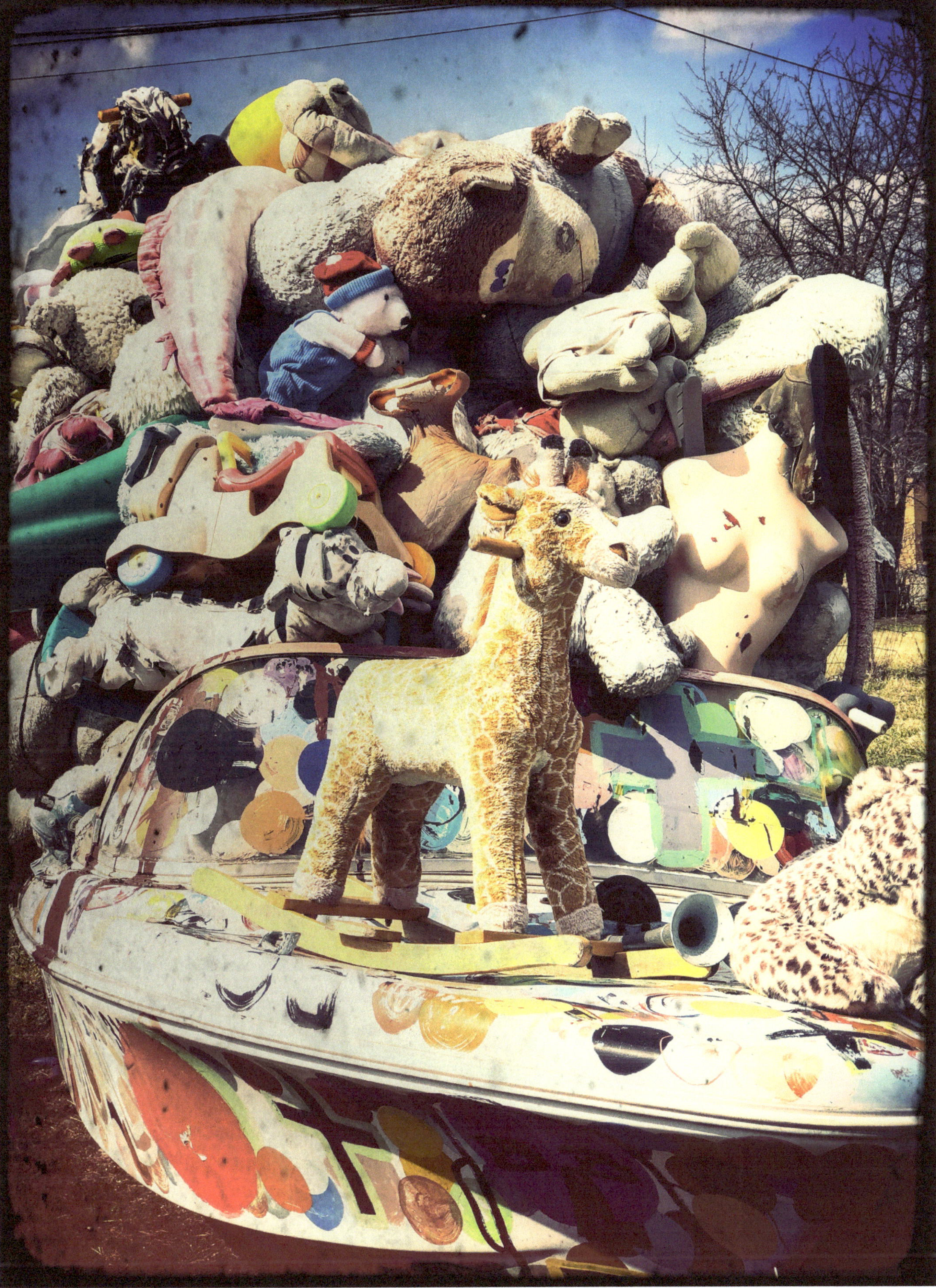

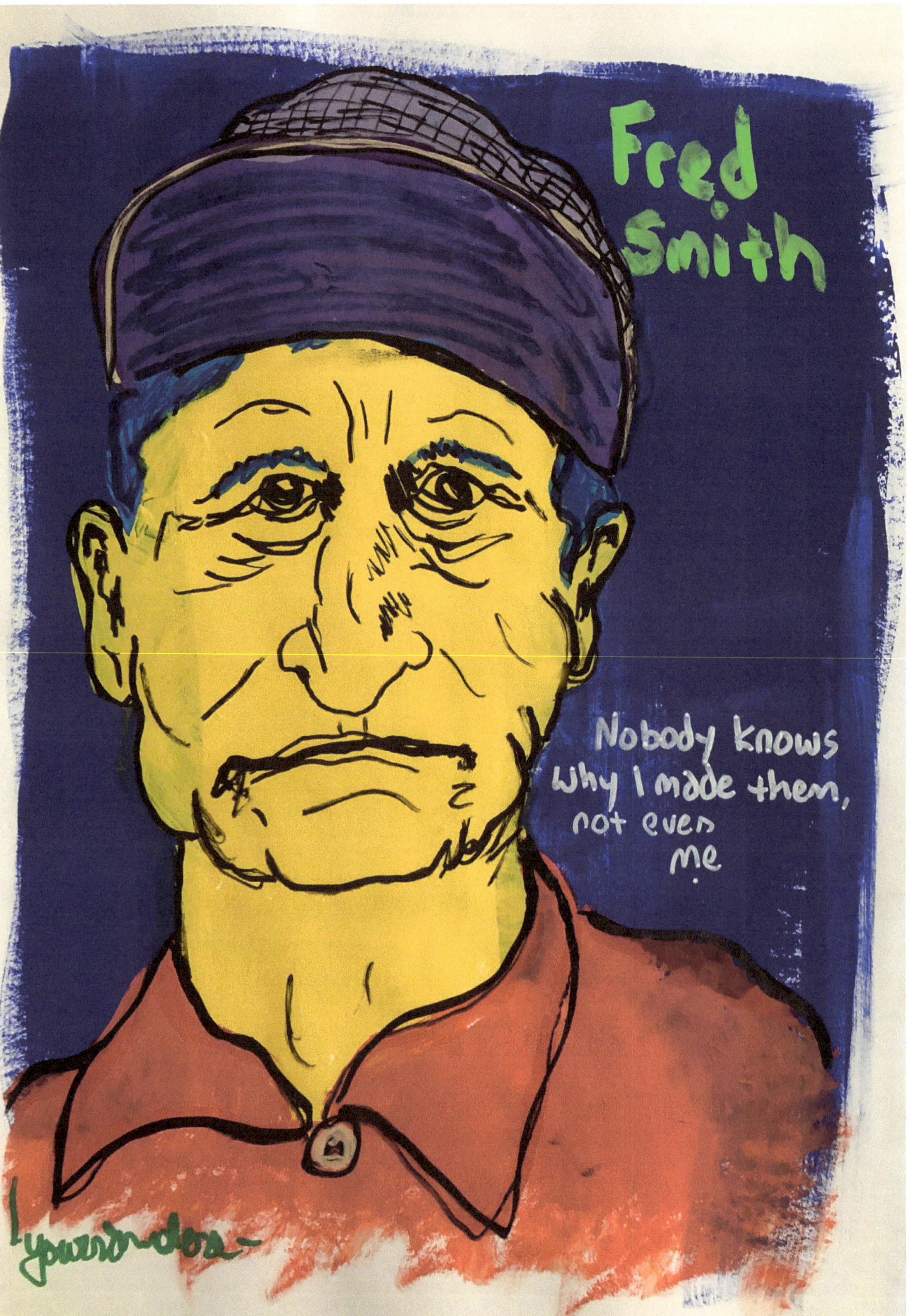

Fred
Smith
Nobody knows
why I made them,
not even
me

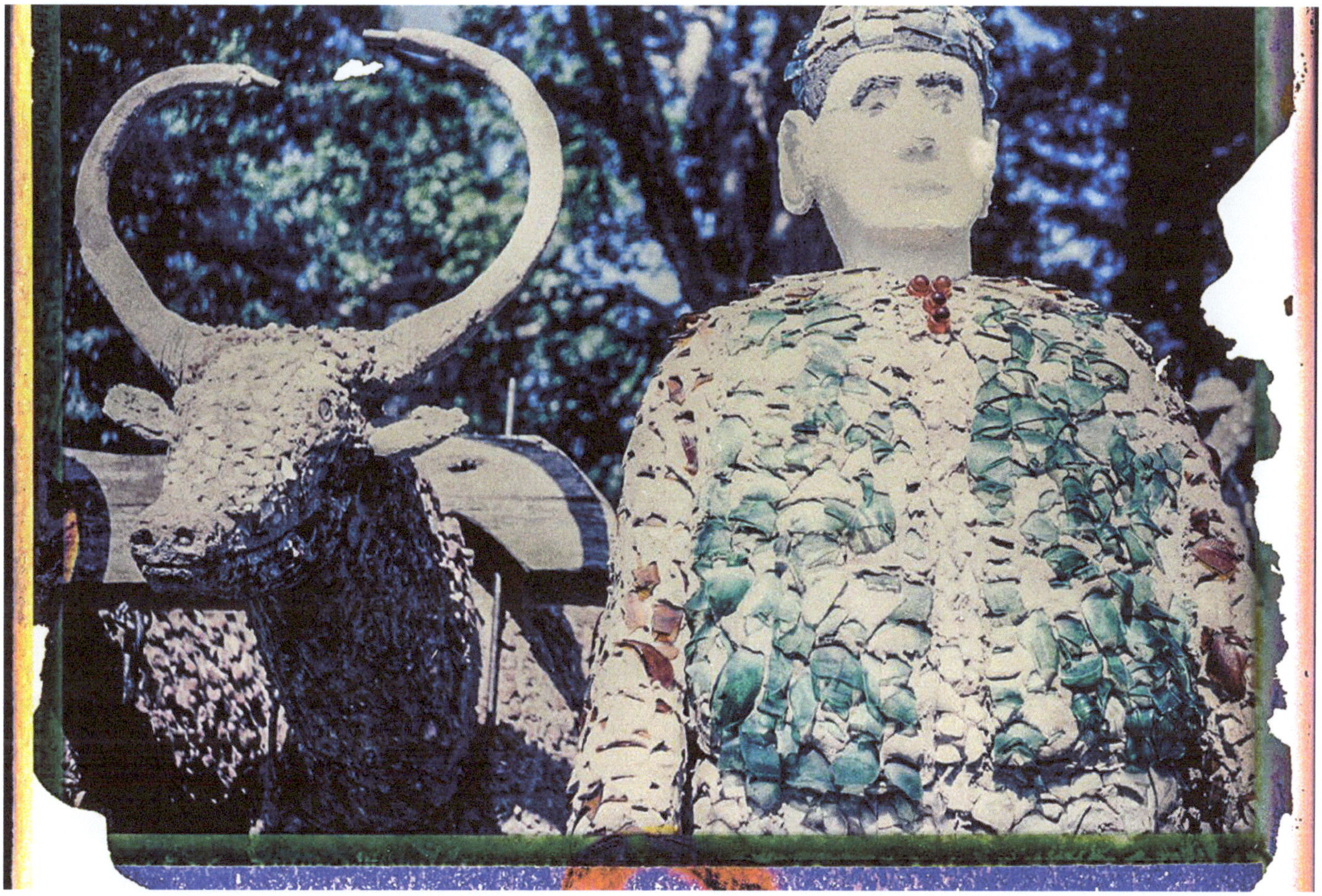

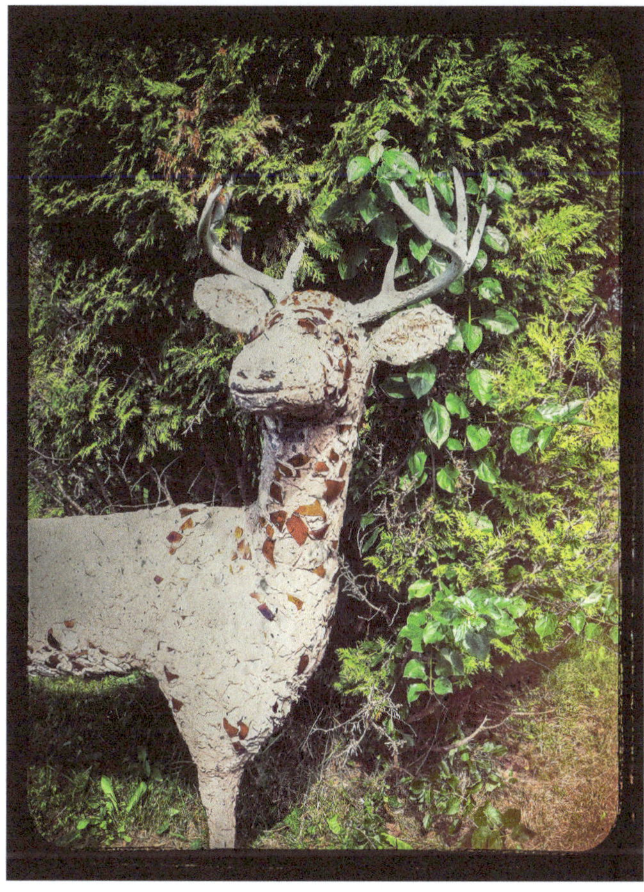

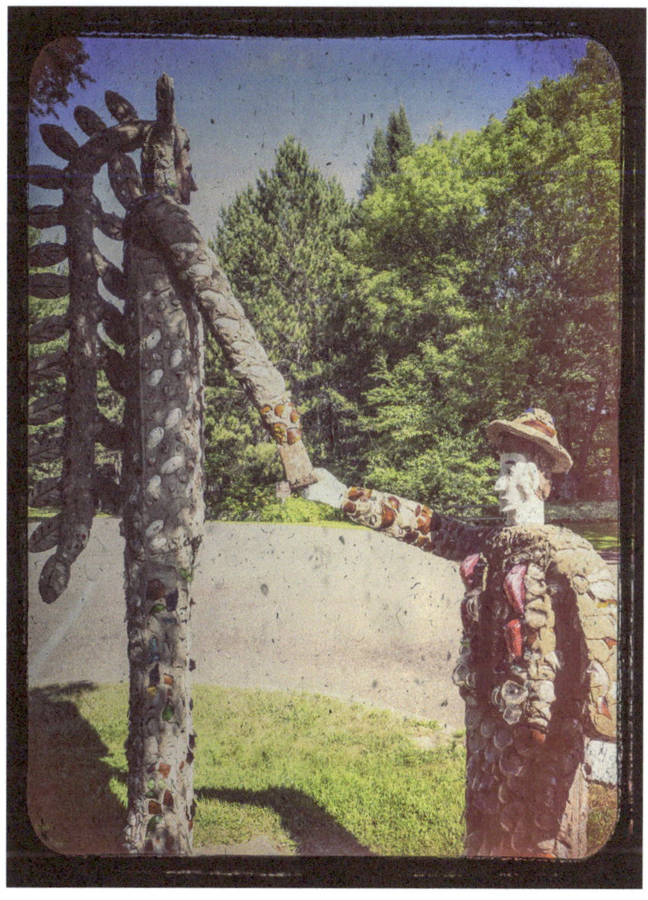

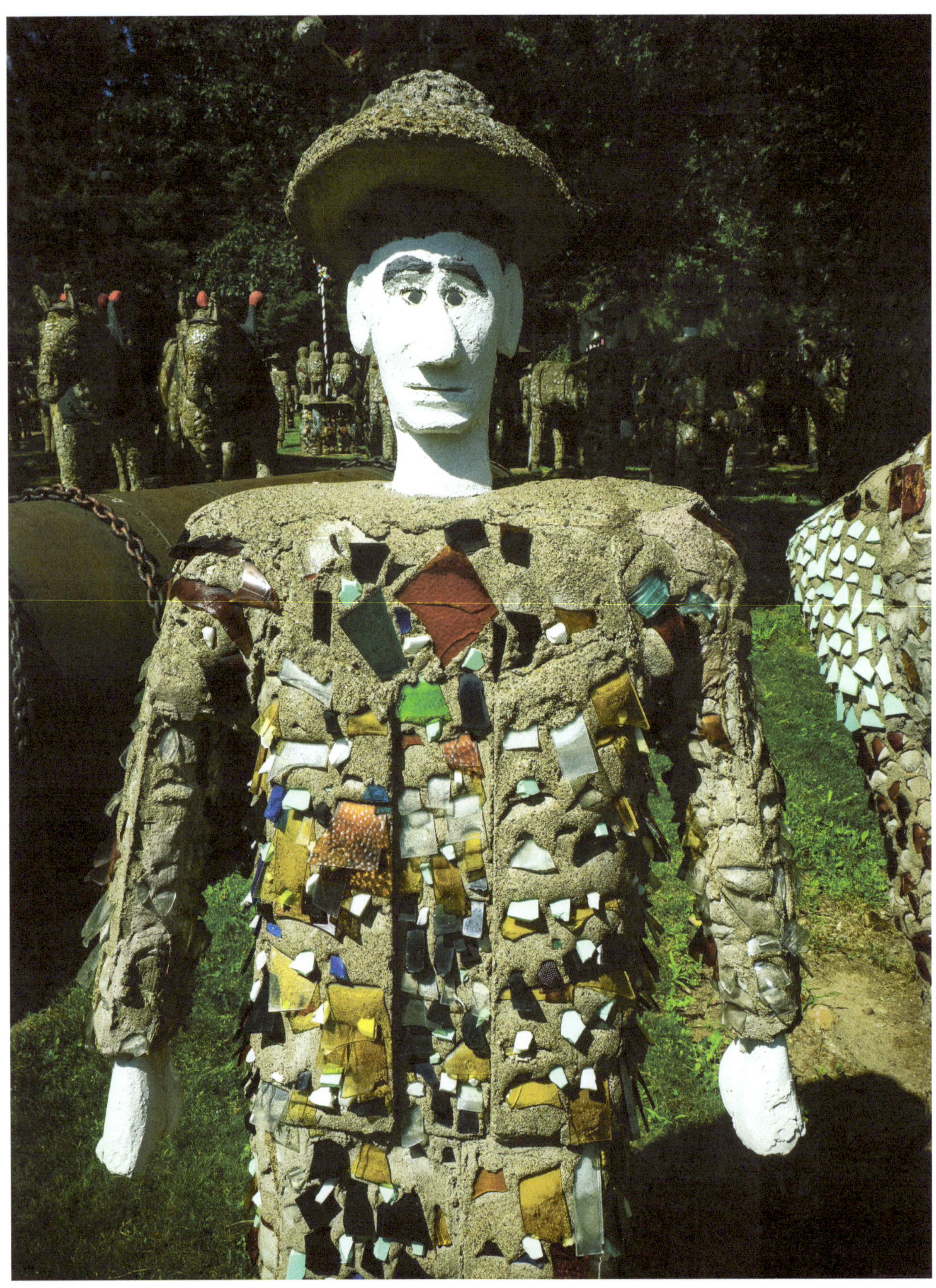

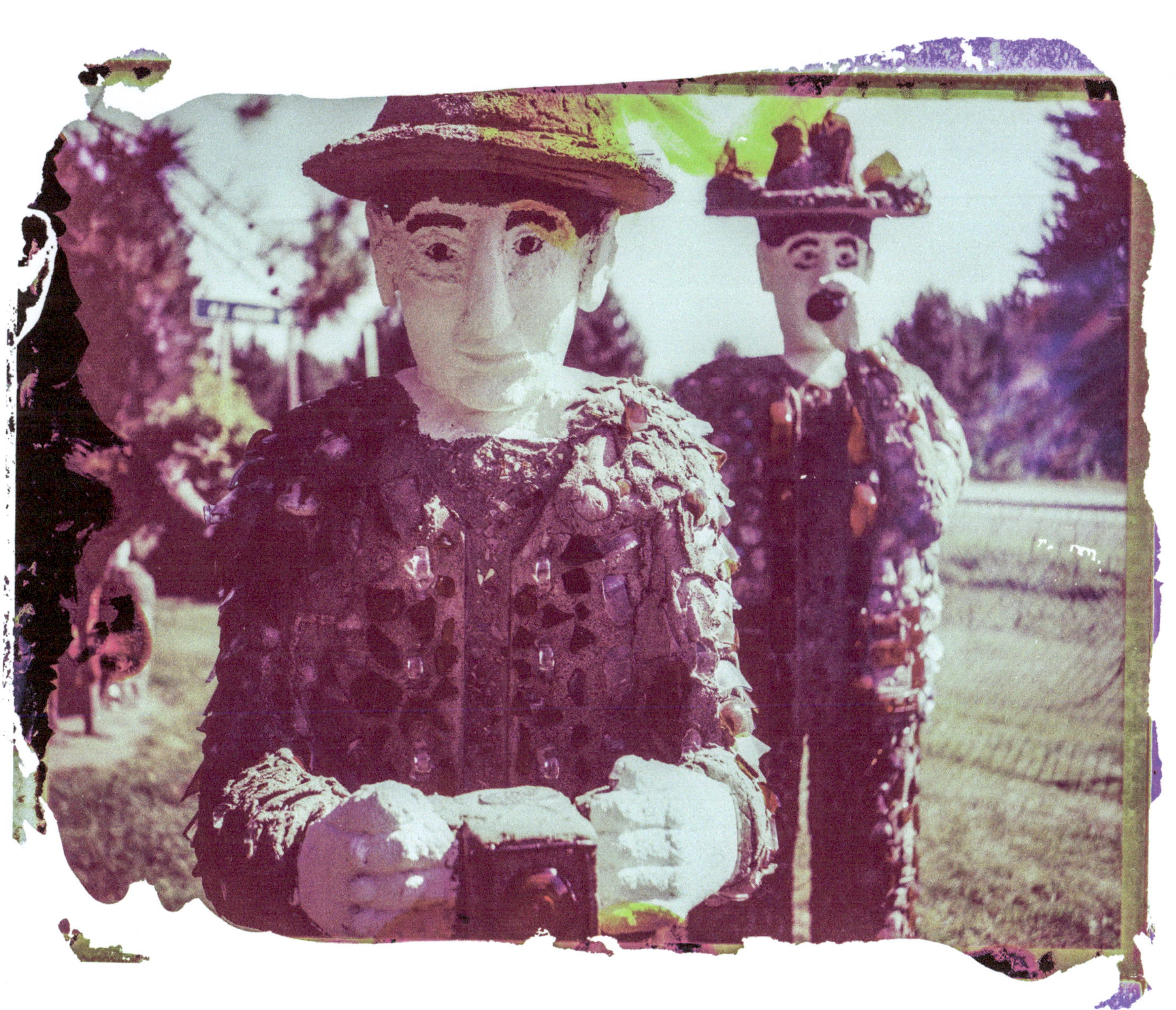

Dmytro Szylak
I don't know what happens when I no longer live ... Maybe it will stay forever.

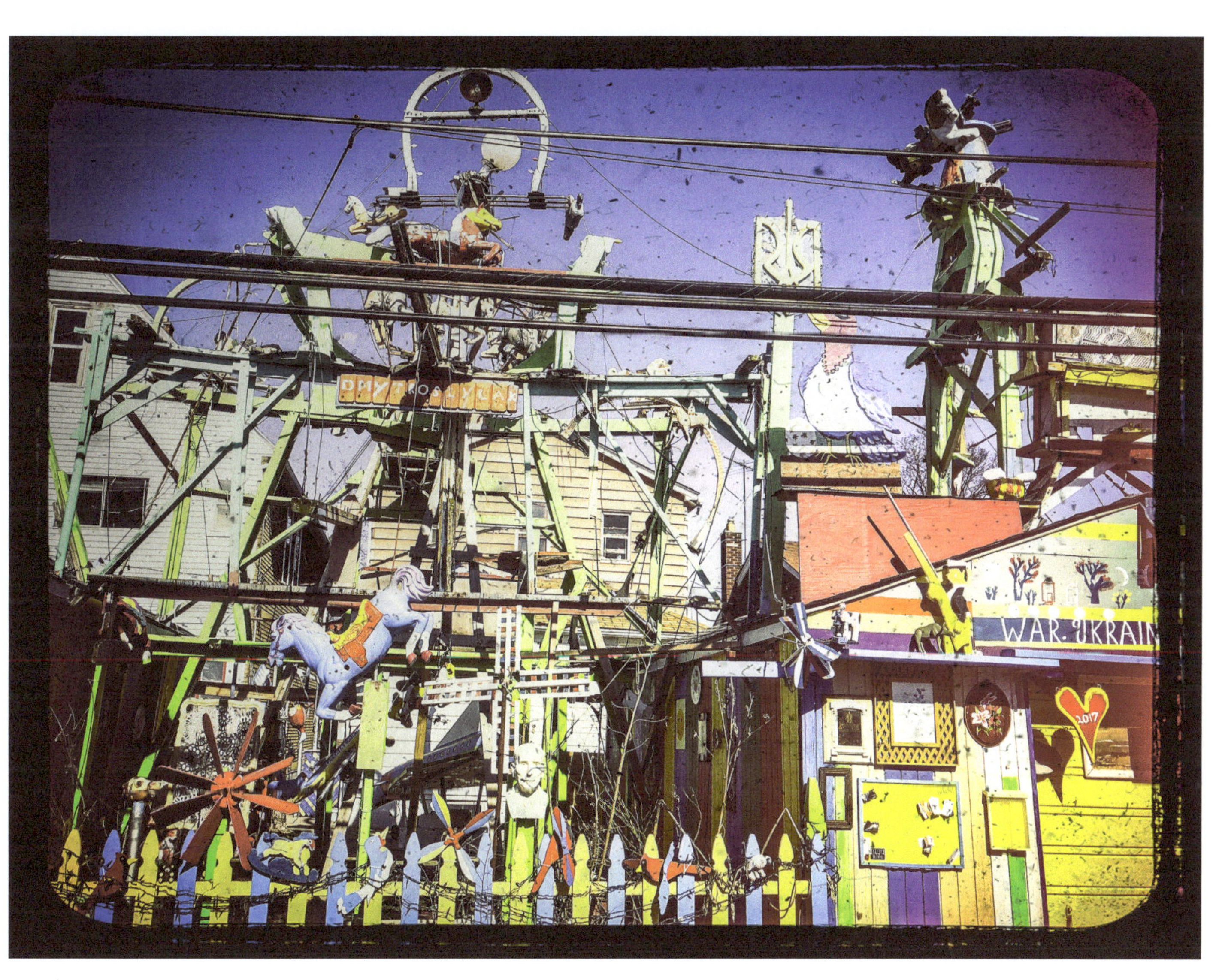
WAR. UKRAIN
2017

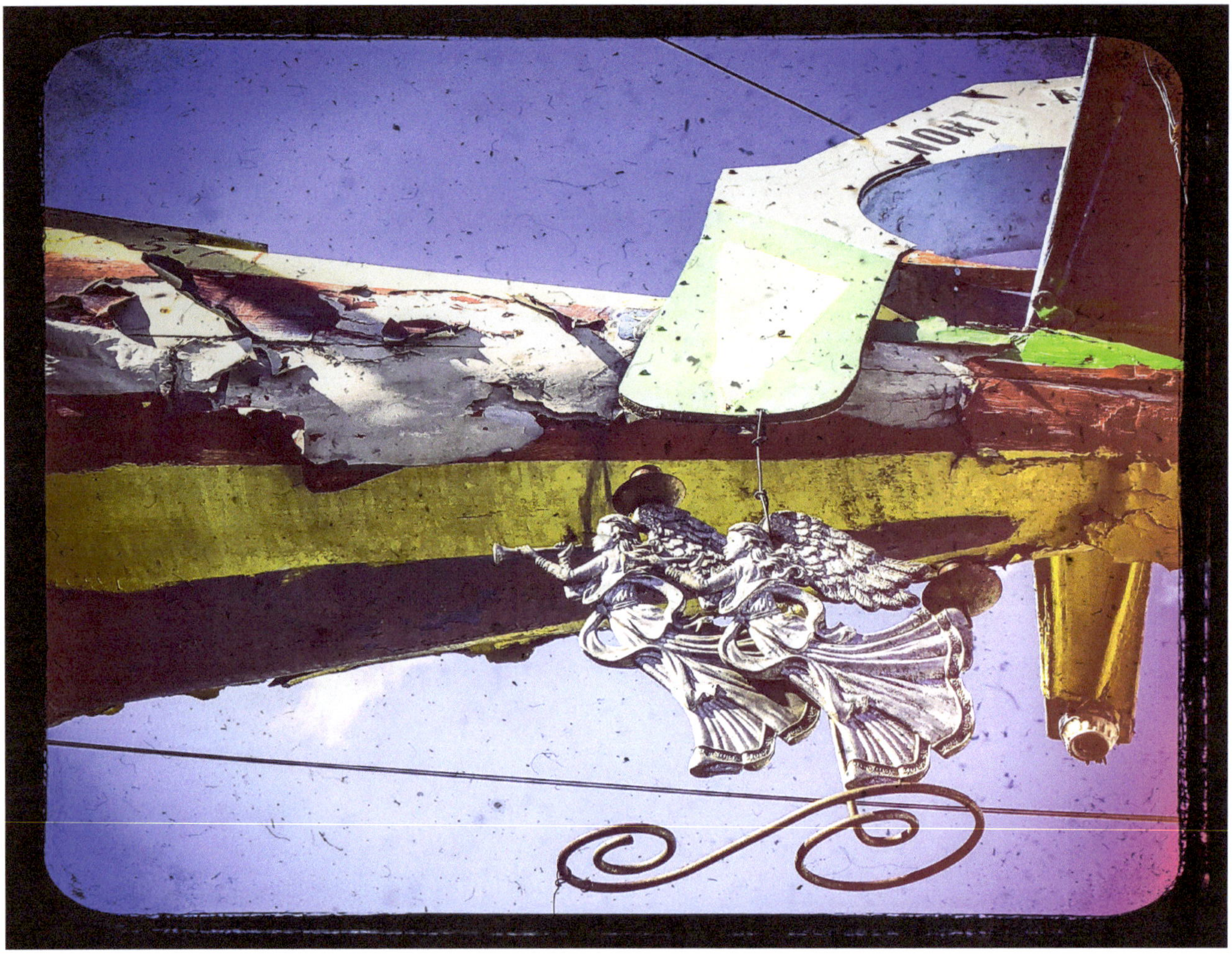

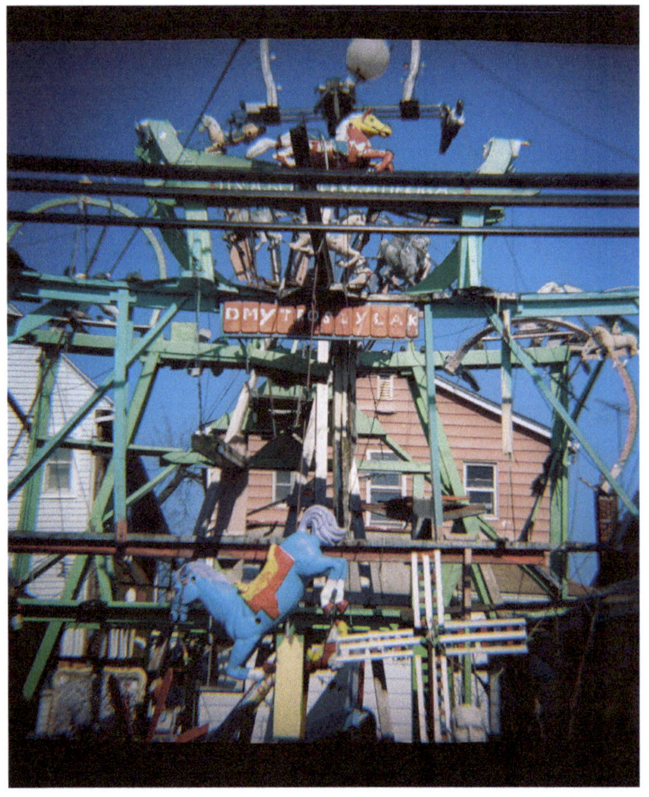

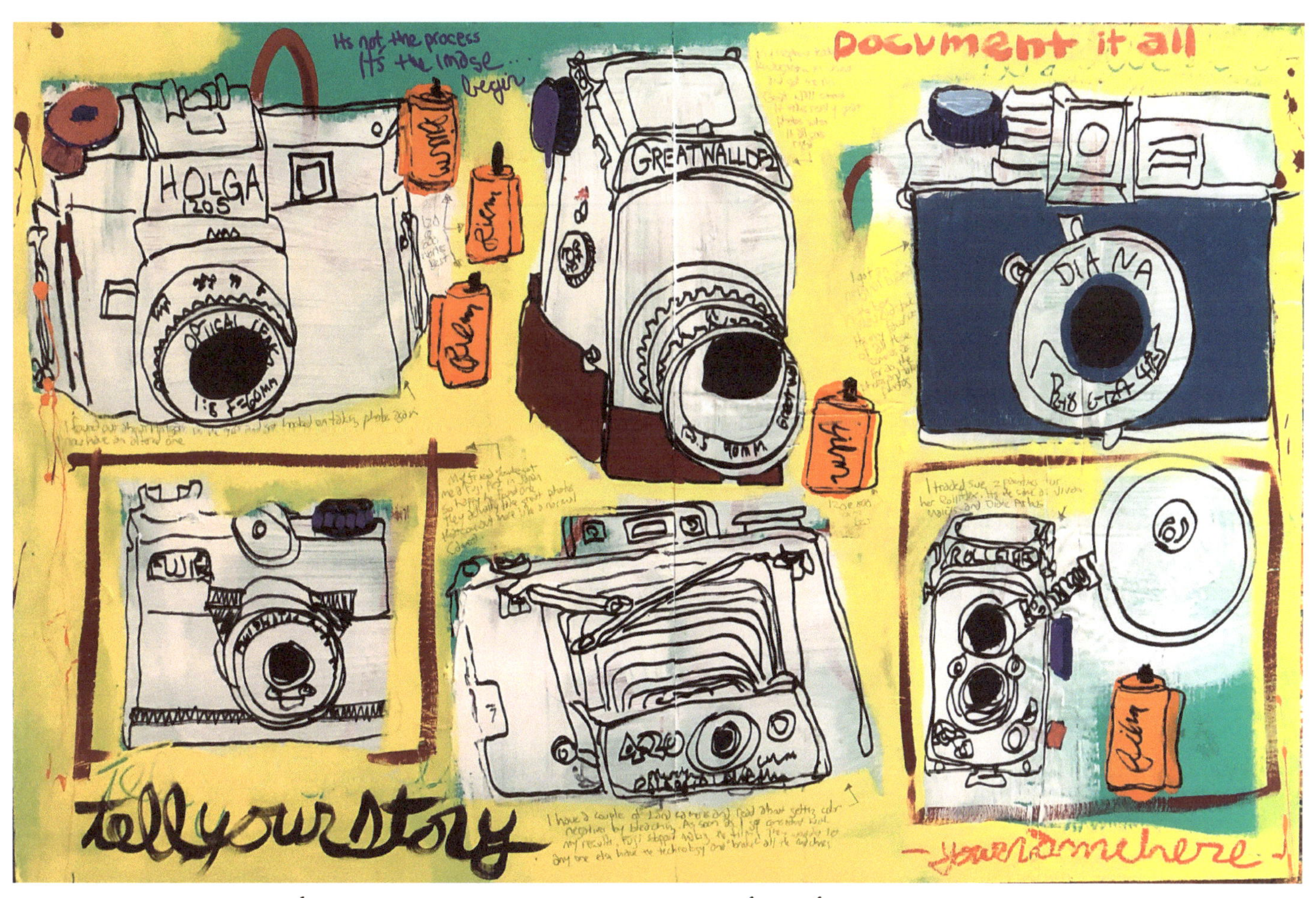

the cameras used for this book
are Diana, Holga, Great Wall & polaroids
and assorted thrift store finds.
The paintings and photos are all by
Tim Kerr
Your name here

Olayami Dabls Detroit MI
African Bead museum
Leonard Knight Niland CA
Salvation Mountain
Mary Nohl Foxpoint WI
Nohl House
M.T. Liggett Mullinville KS
Road Side Field
Noah Purifoy Joshua Tree CA
Outdoor Desert Art Museum
Jeff McKissack Houston Tx
Orange Show
Rev. H.D. Dennis Vicksburg MS
Margaret's Grocery
Howard Finster Pennville/Summerville GA
Paradise Garden
John Milkovisch Houston Tx
Beer Can House
Wash 'Doc' Harris Memphis TN
St. Paul's Spiritual Holy Temple
Eddie Owens Martin Buena Vista GA
Pasaquan
Vollis Simpson Wilson NC
Whirligig Park
Ed Leedskalnin Miami Dade County FL
Coral Castle
Simon Rodia Watts L.A. CA
Watts Towers
Isaiah Zagar Philadelphia PA
Magic Gardens

Dr. Evermor Sumpter WI
Forevertron
Joe Minter Birmingham AL
African Village in America
Samuel P Dinsmoor Lucas KS
Garden of Eden
Billy Tripp Brownsville TN
Mindfield
Clyde Jones Bynum NC
River Critter Crossing
Tyree Guyton Detroit MI
Heidelberg Project
Fred Smith Phillips WI
Concrete Park
Dmytro Szylak Hamtramck MI
Hamtramck Disneyland